Praise for
The Genius of Empathy

"Sharing years of personal insight and wisdom, Dr. Orloff provides her readers with practical advice on how to cultivate a deeper and more sustainable sense of empathy in their lives."

SHARON SALZBERG
author of *Lovingkindness* and *Real Life*

"*The Genius of Empathy* by psychiatrist Judith Orloff is needed now more than ever—our world's empathy deficit has robbed so many people of their health and happiness. This book is an uplifting guide to help heal our minds, soothe our nervous systems, and reconnect us to each other. Highly recommended."

DANIEL G. AMEN, MD
New York Times bestselling author of *Change Your Brain Every Day*

"Dr. Judith Orloff has given us a brilliant book exploring the genius and power of empathy. Only Dr. Orloff could describe the grace of empathy with such exquisite psychological precision. A stunning contribution to our collective healing."

CAROLINE MYSS
New York Times bestselling author of *Anatomy of the Spirit*

"*The Genius of Empathy* is a profound healing approach that takes you on an insightful journey to discover ways to show empathy to yourself and others. Utilizing Dr. Judith Orloff's exercises, you'll learn to navigate both adversity and happiness with compassion. You'll strengthen all your relationships and your connection to the world around you. A must-read for empaths and sensitive souls among us."

ANITA MOORJANI
New York Times bestselling author of *Sensitive Is the New Strong*

"This is a powerful and relatable book to help you unlock your true empathic potential. Dr. Orloff brings her invaluable years of medical training and clinical expertise to this hugely import-ant topic. She guides you step-by-step along the journey to awaken the genius of your empathy."

ALEX HOWARD
author of *It's Not Your Fault* and host of the Trauma Super Conference

"*The Genius of Empathy* will immediately improve your life by helping you to be kinder to yourself and stop overthinking or taking on others' stress. This book will also enhance your com-munication skills, especially with difficult personalities. So many people are craving the kind of healing that Dr. Orloff's caring book offers. Strongly recommended."

IYANLA VANZANT
New York Times bestselling author of *One Day My Soul Just Opened Up*

The
Genius of
EMPATHY

The Genius of EMPATHY

PRACTICAL SKILLS
to Heal Your Sensitive Self, Your Relationships & the World

Judith Orloff, MD

Foreword by His Holiness the Dalai Lama

sounds true
BOULDER, COLORADO

Sounds True
Boulder, CO

This book is not intended as a substitute for the medical recommendations of physicians,
mental health professionals, or other health-care providers. Rather, it is intended to offer
information to help the reader cooperate with physicians, mental health professionals,
and health-care providers in a mutual quest for optimal well-being. We advise readers to
carefully review and understand the ideas presented and to seek the advice of a qualified
professional before attempting to use them.

Some names and identifying details have been changed to protect the privacy of individuals.

Published 2024

Book design by Lisa Kerans

Printed in Canada

BK06479

Library of Congress Cataloging-in-Publication Data
Names: Orloff, Judith, author.
Title: The genius of empathy : practical skills to heal your sensitive
    self, your relationships, and the world / Judith Orloff, MD.
Description: Boulder, CO : Sounds True, [2024] | Includes bibliographical
    references and index.
Identifiers: LCCN 2023029403 (print) | LCCN 2023029404 (ebook) |
    ISBN 9781683649717 (hardcover) | ISBN 9781683649724 (ebook)
    Subjects: LCSH: Self-actualization (Psychology) | Empathy--
    Psychological aspects.
Classification: LCC BF575.E55 O65 2024 (print) | LCC BF575.E55
    (ebook) |
DDC 152.41--dc23/eng/20231107
LC record available at https://lccn.loc.gov/2023029403

LC ebook record available at https://lccn.loc.gov/2023029404

FSC
www.fsc.org
MIX
Paper from
responsible sources
FSC® C016245

To my teacher, Wong Lo Sin See

Out beyond ideas
of wrongdoing and rightdoing,
there is a field. I'll meet you there.

Rumi *(trans. Coleman Barks)*

Contents

PART 3

Healing the World

Foreword

EMPATHY IS one of the most wonderful human qualities. When we are deeply aware of the fundamental truth of our human existence that all of us wish to achieve happiness and overcome suffering, we feel empathy and closeness to them. Compassion, on the other hand, is more than just feeling sorry for someone, because when we are compassionate, we not only feel others' pain, we activate a wish to do something about it. And that gives us courage and inner strength.

Previously it was thought that even positive emotions like empathy just arose spontaneously in response to how others were feeling. Now there is a greater appreciation that such social and emotional skills can be taught and learned. In this book, *The Genius of Empathy*, Judith Orloff offers practical advice on how to cultivate and enhance empathy, which I believe readers will find of great value.

Today, there are eight billion of us human beings, and we all have to live together, so a sense of the oneness of humanity is more necessary than ever before. Cultivating a sense of our common humanity is a way of creating empathy, which can be the basis for creating a happier, more peaceful world.

His Holiness, the 14th Dalai Lama

7 November 2023

Starting the Journey

AS A physician, I'm obsessed with healing.

I've devoted the past thirty years to integrating my conventional medical training—which includes a medical degree from the University of Southern California (USC) and a residency in psychiatry at the University of California, Los Angeles (UCLA)—with my sensitivities as an empath to help my patients heal. In every setting I've worked in, including my private practice, hospitals, nursing homes, and substance abuse programs, I am humbled by the miracle of our bodies' and spirits' capacity to rise like a blazing phoenix above seemingly impossible challenges such as illness, trauma, and loss to begin to heal. What moves me and fuels my passion is identifying techniques that are effective in actionable, real-life terms.

If you're ready for a change that will accelerate your healing process in all areas of your life, empathy is an everyday superpower that is within reach—at work, with family and friends, and in all situations. An empathic life is not about being "saintly" or losing your edge or common sense. Empathy is a practical daily skill that can be learned, not simply an idealistic goal that "sounds good." Its genius is attainable for everyone.

Time and again, I've witnessed empathy's ability to help heal me and my patients. Showing empathy for yourself or receiving it from others can make going through a health or emotional challenge easier. It takes the bite off pain and any conflict as it soothes anxiety, brings mercy to depression, and lets you know you're not alone. You can also get a contact high from other people's joy since empathy helps you live a generous Buddhist sentiment: "My happiness is your happiness. There is no greater happiness in the world." More and more you'll be able to experience this generosity of spirit.

Empathy itself is a healing act, whether you're on the giving or receiving end. It's a way of saying you matter to me, the earth matters to me, being kind to myself and others matters to me. You are not invisible or forgotten. You are seen. You are heard. You are appreciated.

Healing can take many forms, Sometimes, it is physical, but not always. It can be mental, emotional, and spiritual too. Healing doesn't have to mean fully recovering from a health condition, nor is it always equated with a cure. Rather it may be learning to live with chronic pain or illness, for example, in more positive ways. With empathy, you'll bring lovingkindness to healing whether it manifests in small or large ways.

This book focuses on the three main power points of empathy: showing it to yourself, showing it to others, and showing it to the greater world. Empathy is the practice of giving and caring with intention. I'm aware that my well-being and usefulness to others is fueled by being good to you—and also by receiving good from you. That is how empathy flows: both ways.

I wrote *The Genius of Empathy* to support your healing journey. Reading it and using the exercises I suggest will show you ways to approach each day and love yourself through anything, even if you feel lost now. It answers practical questions such as, "How do I have empathy if I'm getting a divorce? If my family treats me unfairly? If I'm overwhelmed or in chronic pain?" The most challenging situation for me is when a loved one is suffering. I'll share what I've learned about coping with this so you can apply it too. I'll go on to provide a road map for how to use empathy at work to improve your communication with coworkers who may be hard to get along with and model grounded ways to support kindness and innovation in your team.

Who This Book Is For

The Genius of Empathy is for everyone who is interested in self-healing and in communicating more effectively in relationships. This book is for all caring people: quiet-loving introverts and empaths as well as extroverts who thrive on stimulation and ambiverts who are a combination of both. It's also for those who may be curious about being more empathic but don't know where to begin. Perhaps your spouse or coworker piqued your interest, so you want to explore.

As part of developing empathy, you'll learn how to avoid absorbing the stress, symptoms, or emotions of others, a skill set that will make you feel safer navigating the world. I offer simple exercises to practice expressing empathy, especially with relationships that are difficult or draining. In addition, I will help you treat yourself with more kindness and stop beating yourself up for perceived shortcomings.

You'll learn strategies to build your empathy in smart, balanced, and comfortable ways. You'll claim your physical, emotional, and spiritual power and take charge of the heartful intention with which you lead your life. Empathy is an expression of goodness that you can be proud of.

This book will also help if you're tired of overthinking problems. Being unable to turn off your thoughts is painful, especially at 3:00 am when you're wide awake and counting way too many sheep. I will describe how to connect to the larger, freer you. It's the part that doesn't need to exhaust yourself by forcing solutions or listening to your monkey mind's incessant chatter, which is jammed with opinions and judgments that don't usually get you anywhere but stuck. My Taoist teacher said about himself,

"Judith, I don't get as bothered by things because I don't think as much as you!" As a physician, I've learned that despite its virtues, the analytic mind alone is too limited to achieve the depth of healing and calm that we all can find.

Though suffering is always an aspect of life—sometimes we have more, sometimes less—I've also watched the victory of how my patients' empathy comforts their suffering. My outlook is that life either brings us blessings or blessings in disguise, at least in some respects. So we can choose to learn from everything. Empathy isn't just "the right thing to do." It can lessen suffering and stop you from waging war with yourself or others. In service to the heart, it is a heroic act.

Empathy softens the struggle, quiets the unkind voices, and lets you befriend yourself again.

I'm fascinated that the word *empathy* comes from the ancient Greek *empatheia*, which means passion or suffering. I agree with the "passion" part but disagree with the stereotype that primarily links empathy with discomfort or feeling overwhelmed. As you'll see, with the proper tools, the "suffering" part becomes optional. Also, empathy has been used to describe how we aesthetically connect with inspiring art or music. I love that because we're each a work of art, and we create our own unique music. Empathy helps us know this about one another.

So, it's with great excitement that I invite you to explore this caring, less-traveled path with me. I am honored to be your guide to help you develop and refine this skill and overcome any obstacles or fears that you might face. This path gets wider and richer the further you go. Also, it's full of surprises and many ah-ha moments that keep you close to your inner wisdom.

I choose to live my life by the codes of empathy and love. I choose to take a deep breath and start again when I lose faith in myself and the world. Every day, I am a student with a beginner's mind—a marvelous, fresh way to live. Come join me on this journey of empathy and the infinite blossoming of your heart.

PART 1

Healing Yourself, Soothing Your Nervous System

1

What Is the
Genius of Empathy?

Becoming the Best
Version of Yourself

WE ARE LIVING IN wild, sacred times.

In this era of polarization, division, addiction, and scarcity, empathy is key to our survival. We are more isolated and lonely than ever. It all can rightfully seem like "too much," and it is—at least, for your logical mind. That's where the genius of empathy comes in. It gives you a wiser, more loving inner resource to guide you and let you view difficulties with more empathic, discerning eyes.

My overriding reason for writing this book is to convey that there is great hope—and that a key to thriving and surviving in these times is empathy. It's never too late to tip the scales toward compassion and goodness. A lack of empathy has helped get us into this personal and global predicament. Reclaiming it will help get us out. Empathy completes our humanity and gives us the strength to seek wisdom beyond the narrow confines of our minds. I'll show you how this is your chance to shine and to see crises as both danger and opportunity, as the Chinese word for crises suggests.

I've called this book *The Genius of Empathy* because it covers a wider territory than how empathy is typically defined. It embraces and goes beyond even our magnificent empathic impulse to be caring with others during stressful times.

I want to give you practical examples of what healthy empathy looks like in the world so you can find it too. This book isn't about staying the same. It's about change and growth and wonder when you lead an empathic life. It's about having room to explore who you really are rather than being limited to the small box your family or society may have put you in.

Choosing empathy is your chance to be extraordinary. It can be such an unexpected action that it changes the rules of tit-for-tat power games and opens new communication breakthroughs. In this book, I'm asking you to be different, to be better, and yes, to change. Instead of simply trying to solve a problem on the problem's level, which doesn't always work, the genius of empathy helps you see from your heart to find the right solutions and perspectives. Becoming empathic leaders and teams, empathic health-care practitioners, and empathic parents, families, and friends will provide exciting new ways to relate to each other. This book is about how to live the empathic paradigm in new and creative ways in daily life.

Empathy is contagious. One act of empathy stimulates another, then another. But you must be the one to initiate it. Practicing empathy each day matters. The smallest of gestures toward yourself, another, or the earth count if you want to shift the energy in your life and the world from war to cooperation. The noble goal is simply trying to understand each other.

Empathy is not something you have to do. The gift doesn't work like that. You have to want it. If you don't, may your chosen path be everything you need it to be. As a healer, my way has never been to try to convince anybody of anything that doesn't resonate for them. However, if you are drawn to empathy or are even slightly curious about how it can enhance your life and relationships so you can stop struggling so much, this book is for you. If you feel stuck or frustrated at home, at work, or in another area, empathy will light the fire of possibility within you to be your best self.

I'm presenting empathy as a skill that you can increasingly develop to navigate both adversity and happiness as compared to sympathy, which is mainly feeling sad for someone's distress. Having empathy for what you're going through offers solace when you feel overwhelmed, in pain, empty, or are losing faith in yourself—and also when you want to revel in the sheer joy of caring and giving. Empathy is the antidote to the frantic state of overthinking and chronic worry. Connecting with your heart can help heal your pain and clutching. Empathy is an energy shifter that starts with you and expands outward to create beneficial change.

But, like some of my patients, you may wonder, *What good will empathy do when my own and the world's problems seem so daunting?* In the following chapters, you will appreciate how powerful it is to simply sit quietly by a candle and search for empathy in your own heart. One person's heart wishing for the good of another is an incredible source of transformation.

The Difference Between Empathy and Compassion

Empathy and compassion are related to each other, but they are different in subtle ways.

Typically, empathy is defined as the ability to attune to other people's emotions, a way of "feeling with them." Empathy is about first connecting to someone's emotions and perspective. For instance, when a friend gets fired, you feel their pain. However, with empathy, you need to learn how to remain attuned to the other person *without taking on their discomfort*. This intimate level of connecting has its own incredible satisfaction and depth.

On the other hand, compassion is when you "feel for" someone and go into action to help. It is more about sending lovingkindness to a person who is suffering than experiencing what they feel. With compassion, you have a bit more distance so you're less likely to absorb others' stress and become drained. On a biological level, compassion signals our hormones and brain chemistry to be of service. So, when your friend gets fired you might find specific ways to support them during this trying time. Your emphasis is on the other person as opposed to your own feelings and responses. Generally, compassion is associated with more ease, whereas untrained empathy can be depleting until you learn strategies to stay centered and enjoy this type of caring too.

Empathy and compassion play a central role in healing. You might find it easy to feel both for people you care about. But I'm also going to take you through various scenarios where empathy and compassion may be harder to find, such as when you don't like someone. I reference both empathy and compassion through-out the book, though I emphasize empathy, which requires a specific skill set to avoid getting overwhelmed by others' stress. Also, compassion is often a response to empathizing with some-one that can spark our impulse to help, but not everyone with empathy is spurred into action. I am fascinated by the unique spectrum of rewards and challenges that empathy offers and how it can enhance compassion in our lives.

Exploring the Genius of Empathy

The scope of empathy goes light-years beyond being a truly "nice thing to do" and how we typically relate to each other. Empathy is a form of emotional intelligence that you can learn and develop. It's a daily healing practice with specific skills that will illuminate every aspect of your life.

This book is a call to action to incorporate empathy into as many situations as possible (your ego permitting!) rather than leaving its role vague or unintentional. It includes what's usually considered empathy, but it also encompasses a fierce, proactive, even radical way of being caring toward yourself, others, and the world, no matter the situation you are facing. Author Maya Angelou got it right when she affirmed, "People may forget what you say . . . but they will never forget how you made them feel."[1]

Cultivating empathy is not about being bland or merely socially correct. Rather, it's a kind of peaceful-warrior training. It entails giving and caring with intention. You will learn to be both strong and loving, neither a pushover nor someone who is rigid. Wherever you are in your life today, this book can meet you there and lift you higher.

Empathy may not be exactly what you think it is. Yes, it's about the tenderness of sharing others' joy and sorrow. Yes, it lets you sense someone's needs so you can help them. But it also is being understanding with those you may not even like and—perhaps much harder—with yourself. As a psychiatrist I know that it is often easier to help others than ourselves.

Empathy is medicine for your mind, body, and soul. It is an alive healing energy that I'll show you how to get in touch with to increase your vitality. It provides a missing element that can calm your nervous system as well as bring harmony and ease to all areas of your life.

Empathy is also a state of openheartedness and warmth that helps you reach for the most admirable part of human nature and the kindness within—while also saying no to bad behavior. It allows you to show respect for others, which sometimes means simply hearing them out or letting them finish a sentence. Plus, it includes spiritual empathy, which connects you with the cosmic forces of love and the great mystery of the universe.

> **A secret to tapping empathy's power is to use the wisdom of both your heart and mind to manifest greater healing.**

Learning to set clear emotional and energetic boundaries so you won't absorb other people's stress is a core part of my teaching. This skill is the foundation of healthy relationships and helps preserve your sensitivities.

For example, as a physician and empath, I want to know, "Where do you hurt?" but I don't want to take on your hurt in my own body. That's a boundary I set for myself so I can work with patients without being depleted. You can do the same while expressing empathy for another.

As part of cultivating empathy, I will also show you how to release the need to always be right, which is a roadblock to your heart. You do this by recognizing empathy's inner opponents of fear, pride, and ego so you can tame them. Then you can relax a little and struggle less. People love hearing, "You know, you might be right," or "I see what you're saying." Acknowledging this is very different from people-pleasing or being untrue to your values. Here, you are consciously choosing to be flexible and affirm someone else's point of view rather than quibbling about minor points or opposing opinions.

Take my friend who was adamant that her daughter's romance was doomed to fail. My intuition didn't agree with her, so I simply replied, "Okay, you seem certain." She smiled and said with gleeful conviction, "I definitely am." So, I let her be right, which delighted her, though her daughter's relationship is still strong a few years later.

It's been said that the highest form of knowledge is empathy because it requires us to suspend our egos and live in another's world. I'm not suggesting that you get rid of your ego. It has strengths too. But, as you'll see, what it wants isn't always best for your well-being. I'll describe how empathy can intervene to create a more positive scenario. Don't let your ego sabotage your heart because it's too stubborn, hurt, or self-righteous to release unproductive behaviors.

Life has challenges. There are many things out there to disturb you. Everyday occurrences such as dealing with a snarky friend, a stressed-out spouse, or rude coworkers may leave you feeling frustrated and tired. Perhaps you've lost your job with no new one in sight. Or you are experiencing depression, anxiety, or physical illness. Maybe the usual methods you've used to feel better aren't working, or they've never fully worked. That's where empathy is the right teacher at the right time.

The genius of empathy is that it allows you to attune to another's wavelength and resonate with where they are at. It's similar to tuning a musical instrument to its purest tone, frequency, and pitch. As a spiritual practice, attuning in this way also connects you more closely to your divine source so you can align with its infinite lovingkindness.

At times feeling empathy is easy: your daughter has a new baby, and you naturally share her bliss. Or a friend's spouse or animal companion is ill, and you offer solace. But in some instances, empathy for yourself and others is trickier. For instance, your friend is about to make the same mistake for the third time, and you become impatient and say something you regret; or your noisy neighbors are disrupting your peace, and you lose your temper when asking them to quiet down. I've struggled to empathize with a friend's choice to stop getting follow-up scans following cancer treatment despite the chance of recurrence. After gently discussing this with him, he said, "Oh, I'll go," but he hasn't acted yet.

Like many of my patients, you might understandably ask, "Why do I want to have empathy for hurtful people or for those who make questionable or destructive choices?" Basically, because it helps free you from any harmful connection with them so you don't nurse a grudge. Carrying around a load of resentments doesn't promote healing.

The type of empathy I'm suggesting lightens your load. Something positive happens when you can show even the slightest empathy for the emotional deficiencies (not the inexcusable behavior) of someone who hurt you. You become freer by releasing your judgments and resentments, even when you are right. Certain people have had so many damaging experiences that "doing their best" for others or themselves may be extremely limited. Still, you don't want to keep them in your head. There are better, more fun thoughts that you can be having. We'll explore all this as we delve deeper into these themes.

Listening to empathy can take you to places you've never been to before or even knew you wanted to go. You're moving toward a magical changing point that has been called the great divide. In geography, this is one of a few locations on earth where rivers change directions on a mountaintop such as the Continental Divide in the Rockies. This ability to reverse or change course has a spiritual counterpoint within you. No matter how far you have fallen or how alone you feel, practicing empathy can recalibrate your path toward healthier ways of behaving and perceiving the world.

Is There a Potential Downside to Empathy?

Despite all of empathy's benefits you may still hesitate to develop it. You may wonder, *Is it possible to have too much empathy and lose touch with my common sense? Does being empathic make me vulnerable to taking on others' pain? I don't want that!* The answer to these questions is yes, but only if you lack strategies to protect and center yourself. Throughout this book, I will teach you how to practice self-care and set healthy boundaries.

> **You must learn to use empathy in balanced ways so you can see people clearly and not burn out.**

Without these skills, you risk becoming a rescuer or a people pleaser where you give too much to the wrong people or overhelp those you love. You may mistakenly feel that it is your job to fix others' problems when it is not. So you become exhausted or feel so much empathy for others' struggles that it clouds your judgment. That's why it's so important to stay centered, clearheaded, and connected to reason too. For instance, if I feel empathy for you, I can express it but not overextend my giving.

Healthy empathy is not about giving endless love to everyone you meet. It involves discernment, checking in with your intuition and energy level, and self-protection. Empathy only becomes problematic if you don't set boundaries, practice self-care, or set limits. Without these techniques, there are no guardrails to hold on to or limitations to keep in mind, and you risk setting yourself up for burnout and empathy fatigue where you have nothing left to give to others or yourself. As a result, you may conclude that empathizing hurts too much, and it's better to stay shut down or numb to protect yourself. However, the impossible price you pay for this choice is to be stuck in your head, living with a closed heart—a fate that is unacceptable to me. The following chapters will show you how to be empathic as well as logically discerning without taking on anyone's drama or pain.

How to Use This Book

I'll present *The Genius of Empathy* from the standpoint of neuroscience, psychology, subtle energy, intuitive medicine, and spirituality to provide a comprehensive understanding of how it works. This is a practical, action-driven guide that shows you how to tap into the healing force in each of us that may need to be activated. You can see empathy at work and in all spheres of your life. It's a learning curve: the strategies I suggest become easier with practice. Each chapter contains stories—from clients and workshop participants (names and identifying details are changed), friends, and me—of learning how to work with empathy more fully. I have included an "Empathy in Action" exercise at the end of each chapter that you can immediately apply to specific situations. Also, in different parts of the book I suggest writing your thoughts and feelings in a journal. So it would be great to have one on hand to complete the exercises I suggest. You will also have the chance to journal spontaneously when topics that interest you come up.

This book builds on the principles of two of my earlier books, *The Empath's Survival Guide* and *Thriving as an Empath,* which teach highly sensitive people and empaths (who don't have the usual emotional filters that others have) to honor their gifts and practice self-care to avoid overwhelm. But here, I'll explore the universal scope of empathy and how it can make our lives and the world a more loving, healthy, fun, and tolerant place.

The Genius of Empathy is divided into three parts; you can read the book in sequence or go to a section that is most relevant to you. This first part, "Healing Yourself, Soothing Your Nervous System," describes the healing power of empathy and presents practices to stop overthinking and come from your heart. There's a self-assessment test to evaluate your current level of self-empathy and enhance this life-sustaining skill. You'll learn what your own "empathy style" is and how it affects your relationships, as well as how to identify obstacles to healing such as emotional triggers, traumas, and fears.

In addition, you'll discover the biology of empathy, including how it can strengthen your immune system and health. You'll learn about the brain's mirror neuron system, which is linked to compassion. It may be hyperactive in high empathy people and lower or absent in those with minimal or no empathy.

In part 2, "Healing Your Relationships," I offer a proactive approach to being empathic without absorbing others' stress or becoming a martyr. You'll practice the high art of empathic listening and holding space for others. You'll become skilled at recognizing people with empathy deficient disorders, which include narcissism and sociopathic personality disorder, as well as people who bully. This will keep you from being lured into the seductive spell of those who simply aren't wired neurologically or emotionally to reciprocate your kindness.

Finally, part 3 expands to "Healing the World." In it, I address empathic leadership in the workplace and around the globe. I'll discuss the healing grace of forgiveness and how praying can activate your "prayer body" to help you find empathy even when you resist it. Finally, empathy will allow you to experience the joy of feeling interconnected with our human family and the natural world with all its miraculous creatures and wild places. Many of us crave this kind of awareness and change. We are whole. We are one on a very basic level. We are a community of souls that can grow together.

Honoring Your True Needs

On your journey of empathy, it's vital to create a life that is in sync with your true needs. For me, this means taking "the road less traveled." I've always been the "outsider" who loves solitude, shies away from parties, and often prefers the company of the ocean or a tree to most people. My whole life, I've talked to the flowers, to the birds, and to the moon. As a child I felt like an alien who didn't belong here. Now, I adore my sensitivities and wouldn't want it any other way.

Whatever your gifts are, releasing shame about feeling different is crucial. I urge you to discard the notion of who others told you to be. Then you can become 100 percent yourself in your views, choices, and sensibilities. Even if you don't know where to start, follow my lead. I'm honored to guide you to that freedom.

I applaud all the freethinkers, creatives, loners, and question-ers of the norm who dare to be true to themselves. I salute all the shy, socially awkward kids who somehow survived the adolescent trials of high school to carve their own paths. I commend every-one who has followed their true extroverted nature and stuck to their vision even when others might have told them to "tone it down" or that their ideas were "too big or unrealistic."

It's liberating to release the idea that something is wrong with you for being different.

What's wonderful about empathy is that it can benefit all kinds of people: those who prefer being insiders or outsiders, empaths or nonempaths, conventional or nonconventional, and anyone in between. Perhaps you don't identify with any category, and that's fine. Empathy can improve all our lives and relation-ships. Some of my patients are outgoing movers and shakers in the world who use empathy in the workplace and their personal lives. Unlike me, they don't require lots of alone time, and they flourish being around large groups of people. There are many ways to embody empathy that can uniquely suit each individual.

• ● •

Feeling empathy is the joining point of all bridges going to all places —a coming together of heart and mind. When I am experiencing empathy, I want to breathe fully, I want to be still and let my heart be filled with empathy's grace and warmth. This is the language of my heart, but we all may experience empathy differently. You may not be an intense feeler like me. The rest of this book will help you find your own way, your own words, and your own benefits of empathy.

As I'll describe, there are compelling intellectual, emotional, and spiritual reasons to develop your empathy, including the prospect of healing parts of you that may have been in pain longer than you might like to admit. Maybe it's time to release even the justified grudge festering in your gut so you can be free of that burden. Perhaps you can start gauging your success each day by the number of heartfelt connections you make rather than anything material. Or you can start focusing on a future of wonder rather your scars from love's wounds. You deserve another chance and a fresh start.

The world is full of good arguments about why we can't find empathy and peace in our own lives or in the tumultuous world. Consider all the people there are with empathy deficient disorders such as rampant narcissism and bullying. You might ask, "With these deterrents, how can we possibly love each other or get along?" The answer comes from your heart, not from your head or from all the logical evidence you can accumulate about human nature's deficiencies. Empathy offers a path out of misunderstanding and hate. This is my simple focus. To find empathy, a starting place is for your heart to connect with others who value having an open heart too.

Empathy will keep us all bound together; not warlike but tolerant and curious and embracing both our similarities and our differences. That's why I'm so drawn to it, despite all the "logical" reasons not to be. Year after year, I keep letting empathy expand my practice of medicine, the way I listen to my patients' needs, and my own life. *Empathy is the best of what it means to be human.* May actualizing this be our purpose—to heal and to love in the midst of adversity and embody a greater optimism. Let me help you get there and experience your finest hour. Once you discover that grace, it will never leave you as long as your heart keeps searching for it.

Your Initiation into Self-Healing

The time has come to begin again. Commit to being kinder to yourself, more tolerant, and more forgiving. Start to kindle the healing energy of empathy. If you are hurting and want to mend your body, mind, or spirit, inwardly make a sincere request to initiate the process. Affirm, *May I be happy, well, and unburdened of worry*. Then, with a humble heart, get ready for this new path to unfold.

2

Igniting the Healing Power of Empathy

How to Stop Overthinking and Come from Your Heart

SOMETHING BEAUTIFUL is about to happen.

Prepare for a positive shift.

You will be filled with more life from this.

Like many people, you want your time on this planet to be meaningful. You want to be appreciated, loved, and understood. When I look back from my last day here, I want to feel love and remember the simple, soulful things—a spring hike in the canyons with a friend, a quiet writing day, a hug from my partner, the warmth of my workshop participants sitting in a circle exploring their souls. I know I will remember the kindness and empathy others have shown me and that I have been graced to show others.

So, who do you want to be? What do you want to remember in your final moments, when the space between here and the unknown is bridged only by an arc of twinkling stars and a smile from the universe telling you everything will be okay? Even if your life was filled with what seems like an inordinate number of hardships, I doubt that you want to be consumed with the hollow sense of bitterness, revenge, and resentments in the end; though of course, that would be your right. Also, the desire to accumulate wealth and worldly power will be worth nothing then. I invite you to identify what is truly meaningful to you, no matter how small: the flashes of love from your child, the kindness of a stranger, or a friend who keeps you company when you are ill. Pinpoint what values and positive beliefs have supported you in good times and bad, the sustaining experiences that live on in your heart.

Who we are, the type of people we want to grow into, makes a huge difference in our capacity to heal and in our happiness. Simply trying to be a good person—for instance, someone who values love, kindness, and service—is a healing act, though it can be harder than you think. We want to get along with each other, which may seem like a formidable task without empathy.

Since fear fuels hatred and division, a requisite for empathy is to keep healing our fears. This lets us honor the experiences of all people. I am touched by what civil rights leader Rosa Parks said when asked if she was angry at the past: "No, if you stay angry at other people you might miss finding friends among those you were angry with."

Welcome to the world of empathy and the heart. It offers many creative ways to be happier and address difficult scenarios in your life from a kinder, more conscious place. I smiled when one workshop participant said, "I teach my children and grand-children that empathy is a secret ingredient in grandma's recipes to understand people and live well."

Life can be uncertain. You never know what it will ask of you or who you will meet. Every person, every annoyance or delight can teach you to become a more empathic person.

As rugged or joyous as life can be, it offers valuable lessons about how to heal and bring empathy into each situation.

The Emergence of Your Larger Self

To develop empathy, the first step is to understand that we each have a small and a large self. The small self is limited to the personality level where your ego, intellect, and emotional struggles dominate, and the large self is ruled by the heart. The small self is strong on logic and analyzing situations, which are both great assets, but the mind can be both a friend and an enemy. It is also prone to insecurity, arrogance, pride, fear, and anxiety and lacks the tools to rise above them. Thus, the small self has a restricted vision of what's possible.

I know how painful it can be to stay stuck in an overactive mind, a state that reminds me of Bruce Springsteen's song about a freight train going through his head. The mind's chatter can drown out everything else. Plus, it goes nonstop and keeps you stuck in circular thinking. Meanwhile, the small self compellingly tries to argue you out of empathy and offers "good reasons" to cling to suffering, fear, and grudges. Here are some ways to change that.

Nine Strategies to Combat Overthinking

1. Compassionately identify the unproductive pattern.
2. Focus on breathing through your nose to shift out of your mind and into your body.
3. Kindly tell yourself, *Overthinking won't help resolve the problem. It only frustrates me.*

4. Focus only on the Now rather than making up scary stories about the future. Do this by focusing on your breath, the physical details of where you are sitting, what you are wearing, how you are feeling, and only on problems that need to be solved today rather than those that may or may not come tomorrow.

5. Accept what you do have the power to change rather than dwelling on situations beyond your control.

6. Gently put your hand over your heart or simply focus on this area and visualize an uplifting image that relaxes you such as the ocean, a bouquet of roses, or a seagull floating in the sky.

7. Keep repeating, *All is well. With time, this issue will be solved.* Or simply *Ohm*, which in Sanskrit means "I am peaceful."

8. Listening to serene music transports you out of your mind and into your heart. Some of my favorites are Wah!, Enya, and Bach. Find a playlist that makes you happy and relaxed or reconnects you to the magic of life. Or you might like music that makes you dance. Music has the power to heal an overactive mind by shifting your focus from worry and problem-solving to happiness, beauty, and fun. It's impossible to "think" the experience of music. You must feel it.

9. An antidote for overthinking or overtalking is to revel in the wonder of nature: a sunset, a dusky dawn, a sliver of moon, trees swaying in the breeze . . . whatever touches you. If you're near an ocean or a body of moving water such as a waterfall or creek, take in the relaxing negative ions that water in motion emits. Also, focus on the tranquil sounds of the wind or birdsong.

(Or you can get an app that plays thunderstorms, rain, or the sound of the surf.) Open a window, go outdoors, or simply concentrate on these glories of nature to quiet your thoughts.

Overthinking is harder to quell when your ego can't let go. It gets hurt and stays hurt. It would rather be right and have you remain stressed and angry than for you to release those burdens. This outlook can make you into an unhappy person. You may grow tired of repeating the same story but don't know how to stop. Also, it's a turnoff to keep rehashing with friends, kids, or grandkids how someone has wronged you. They will get tired of listening.

I have a colleague who has clung to a horrible financial betrayal from thirty years ago. He will not hear of letting go of his resentment (though I've broached the possibility with him) and will eagerly repeat the incident to anyone who will listen. I cringe when I hear him starting up and quickly move out of earshot. Certainly, he has the right to be angry, hurt, and resentful. But for all these years, those feelings have churned inside him. Is that what you desire for yourself? Stored-up resentments are poison. They mainly harm you.

Unfortunately, many people unknowingly live much of the time in their fearful, worried, smaller self and don't see the way out—or even know there is one. But you will. You'll learn to inhabit your larger self: the compassionate, intuitive, empathic parts that can access a greater source of wisdom and Spirit. Beyond your mind's chatter and fears, you're in a timeless space. You're not as influenced by the small self's expectations and concerns, so empathy is more available.

In your heart-centered large self, you can be more loving with yourself and better understand others. But if you're only operating from your logical mind, you might not even know that another perspective exists. You are stuck in one reality, but we can be so much more.

As a daily empathy exercise to access your large self, ask yourself, *How can I come from my heart, not just my head?* This alerts your mind that you are doing something different. The mind need not fear that it's being replaced. Rather, you're giving it a friendly companion. Your heart and mind can work as a tag team. Sometimes you need logic; other times you need heart; or you may need both. Many people are unhappy and don't see a way out because they don't know how to consciously cultivate their hearts. Learning this skill is life-changing.

Empathy is the way of the heart. It lets you switch channels out of your busy mind to a different frequency where healing can happen.

Once you shift out of your intellect and ego, loving forces can offer extra help. With an open heart you may become willing to consider, *Perhaps there's a better choice that I'm unaware of. Perhaps I can change my attitude or behavior to heal a relationship.*

I'm asking you to take part in the experiment to experience the genius of empathy and reimagine your capacity for kindness. It will challenge you to rise above the ego's logical reasons to stay small, rigid, and bitter or to overthink. This shift may feel strange, uncomfortable, or even undoable at first. That's okay. I'll lead you through the specific steps of this process. When you stretch, it's natural to encounter resistance. Go slow. Stay with it. The freedom you'll experience will help you approach life from an easier, more satisfying position.

I am inspired by the classic ancient Taoist text *The Art of War* by Sun Tzu, a mysterious Chinese warrior and philosopher who lived over two thousand years ago. His teaching is as much about war as it is about peace and how to best resolve our conflicts with each other.

Sun Tzu wrote, "To solve a conflict without fighting is best; accomplish the most by doing the least."[1] His revolutionary approach doesn't endorse arguing or going to battle as the optimal solutions to problems large or small. Instead, strategizing and "knowing your enemy" are key rather than simply reacting with malice or frustration. He believed that war is only a last resort, and we must always be miserable (never celebratory) about this option. Also, he warned that we can be used by our egos to aggravate conflicts with people or within ourselves. The ego typically wants to "get back at" others rather than find more positive, enduring solutions. So, in the spirit of empathy, we begin our adventure into the wiser, larger parts of ourselves.

As Sun Tzu suggests, I want to lead my life according to the art of peace. What does this mean? First, we can all gradually stop punishing and fighting with ourselves. Second, we must stop harboring resentments or hatred because they are "deserved"—a topic we'll explore later. Third, empathy doesn't mean dancing around someone's bad behavior or trying to play "nice." Rather, as a warrior, it's learning to claim your power by setting firm boundaries with mindful, swift action.

Also, in my life, I don't want to be constantly aggravated and exhausted by letting others trigger my anxieties, anger, or self-doubts. I am not interested in high drama or inciting conflict just to appease my hurt feelings or areas of low self-esteem. Rather, I choose empathy as my guide, even when my ego is screaming, *Choose me, keep arguing, stay at war* and my heart is saying, *Let's find peace.* As tempting as the ego's plea to retaliate or hunker down in hurt feelings or resentments may be, my being yearns to take a wider, more loving path.

Choosing empathy is a game changer. It gives you the option of living in a more spacious, heartfelt part of yourself. Then you can see every situation, from trauma to happiness, from the most compassionate, "big-picture" place. It's not about trying to placate or make excuses for an adversary. It involves understanding them, while also saying no to their behavior, ideally without a fight. Sometimes it means eliminating someone from your life. To achieve this level of personal power, you must pause and plan how to respond from your best instincts.

To generate empathy in a range of situations, including work, intimacy, family, and friendships, you'll need to access the wisdom of both your head and your heart. I feel happy imagining these two parts of us as good friends holding hands rather than as opposing forces, as conventional medicine often portrays them.

With empathy you'll find balance, neither overthinking a situation nor feeling so intensely that you take on others' stress and are overwhelmed. You won't be stuck in the spin cycle of a busy mind. You can stay centered in even the most heated moments.

The sacred pause is the first step toward shifting into your larger empathic self despite all the tempting urges you may encounter not to do so.

The Wisdom of Slowing Down: Practicing the Sacred Pause

As part of empathy training, get in the habit of pausing when you are agitated so you can respond from your best self.

If you feel upset, take a few moments to stop and calm down. Do not react, impulsively respond, or say something you'll regret—no emails, texts, or calls, especially if you are hungry, tired, or busy. Take a deep breath to center yourself. Take another few breaths to ease into the pause. Now, for a few quiet minutes slowly breathe, relax, and tell yourself, *Everything will be okay. I can handle this.* The sacred pause is a time to regroup, show yourself kindness, and shift from your small self to your large self.

The Four Styles of Empathy

How we attune to ourselves or others may be different for each of us depending on which of the four styles of empathy—cognitive, emotional, intuitive, and spiritual—we relate to most strongly. You can get to know the way you are wired by identifying your primary empathy style (though you may relate to other styles too). Your main style is your default setting, how you naturally express empathy most of the time. Knowing your style is the starting place to appreciating how your own empathy functions and how you can comfortably give and receive caring. (Note that people with narcissistic personality disorder and others who have empathy deficient disorders don't have an actual style of empathy because they lack this quality.)

All styles of empathy can be healing in their own ways. The goal is to make the most of your assets and also experiment with different styles to broaden your options. You may relate to more than one style. For instance, my primary style is intuitive empathy, though I enjoy incorporating cognitive empathy, which is more cerebral, and other types as well. I like having choices in how I respond.

Review the descriptions of the four styles of empathy below to get a greater understanding of which styles you relate to as well as their associated benefits and challenges.

Style 1. Cognitive Empathy: The Thinker/Fixer

If your primary empathy style is cognitive, you're most comfortable with a concrete, cerebral approach to emotions. Consider this style "thinking empathy." You use your mind to understand others and wish the best for them. You are solution oriented. You want to logically fix a problem with brain power but are frustrated if you can't. You may respond to a friend in distress with, "I understand that this situation is hurtful, and here's what you can do about it" rather than, "My heart feels for you," and then give them space to express their discomfort.

Many physicians show cognitive empathy so they can stay emotionally neutral and just stick to the case's facts. They prefer analyzing a patient's pain or dis-ease through test results and technology rather than also attuning to their own feelings and intuitions or helping patients process theirs. During an office visit, they may be glued to their computers taking notes rather than simply listening.

If you have cognitive empathy, you might be drawn to being an attorney, a linearly oriented physician, an engineer, a computer programmer, a banker, a financial analyst, an accountant, a property inspector, or a detective.

Advantages

- You're calm in a crisis.

- You're a brilliant analyzer.

- You keep an emotional distance so you do not get overwhelmed by intense feelings or risk losing yourself in other people.

- You offer practical solutions.

Disadvantages

- You risk seeming cold or detached.

- To protect yourself from feeling too much, you may disconnect from your own emotions or another's.

- You offer solutions too quickly before someone fully expresses their feelings.

- You get exhausted from overthinking.

Finding Balance: Feel More, Fix Less

Try this approach to improve your empathic communication in relationships and get in touch with your emotions. If someone comes to you upset or in tears—for instance, your spouse is distraught about work or the kids, or a friend is worried about finances—simply say with kindness, "I appreciate how you're feeling," rather than rushing to fix the problem. For at least a few minutes, just listen. This aligns you with them empathically so they can feel heard. Then you can suggest possible remedies.

Similarly, when you're upset, first show yourself kindness before prematurely forcing answers. This leads to more heartfelt resolutions.

Style 2. Emotional Empathy: The Feeler

If your primary empathy style is emotional, you empathize with others through your emotions. Consider this style "feeling empathy." You have a big heart and are responsive to people's needs. You feel everything, but sometimes to an extreme. Like me and many other sensitive empaths, you may be an emotional sponge whose body absorbs others' distress as well as their joy. Since emotions can be contagious, you are vulnerable to catching them.

Neuroscience links emotional empathy to the brain's mirror neuron system, which generates compassion by mirroring other people's emotional states. If a friend is hurting, you hurt. If a family member is content, you feel content. It is natural to say to others, "I feel your pain. I care about you." As an empath, my heart aches along with loved ones when they are going through hard times. Similarly, you are emotionally present with people, and they feel your caring.

If you have emotional empathy, you might be drawn to the creative arts and the helping professions, including being a psychotherapist, a social worker, a nurse, a coach, or a massage therapist. Also, you may go into teaching, human resources, or the clergy or volunteer in nonprofit organizations, animal rescue, or other heartfelt causes.

Advantages

- You are loving and compassionate.

- You're a good friend, partner, and coworker.

- You're passionate about helping others.

- You make people feel seen and heard.

Disadvantages

- You are overwhelmed by too many feelings.

- You get tired from overgiving and people-pleasing.

- You have difficulty setting healthy boundaries.

- You neglect your own needs and worry excessively about others.

Finding Balance: Set Clear Boundaries

To be comfortable with emotional empathy, use these strategies to stay centered and stop taking on people's stress.

- **Repeat this affirmation inwardly or aloud:** "It is not my job to take on other people's pain. I can be caring without exhausting myself." As a reminder, say this at least once daily to cue into your power and not overgive. It's fine if you need to "fake it" until you can fully live the statement's message.

- **Practice setting healthy boundaries:** "Boundaries are the distance at which I can love you and me simultaneously," says teacher Prentis Hemphill.[2] If someone asks more than you can give, learn to say positively, "No" or "Not now." Politely, even graciously, tell them in a kind, firm tone, "I'm sorry, I'm unable to do that." Keep remembering, "No" is a complete sentence. Be succinct rather than getting defensive or overexplaining. This form of self-healing will protect you from getting overwhelmed by others' needs.

Style 3. Intuitive Empathy: The Subtle Senser

If your primary empathy style is intuitive, your keen intuition and sensitivity let you read people and their nonverbal cues more easily. Consider this style "sensing empathy." Your intuition senses if someone is being authentic or if they aren't. You have strong gut feelings, ah-ha insights, knowings, or dreams. You also feel the positive and negative vibes that people emit. These vibes come from what Chinese medical practitioners call "chi," or subtle energy, which extends inches or feet from the skin.

For a subtle senser, the energy someone radiates communicates volumes about them. Albert Einstein believed that everything is energy. Some energy is healing, some is not. For instance, you sense a friend's creative excitement about their film project and receive a boost in your body. Similarly, your positive vibes can uplift them. Or you may sense that someone is struggling despite their outer smile, and their stress jangles you. The invisible language of subtle energy helps you interpret your environment and is a natural way for you to empathically give and receive.

If you have intuitive empathy, you may be drawn to being an artist, a designer, a filmmaker, a musician, a teacher, or a healthcare provider. You might love working with plants, flowers, or animals or preserving the health of marine life and the oceans.

Advantages

- You have strong intuition and an open heart.

- You are attuned to the subtle vibes of people, places, and nature.

- You are able to read others' needs.

- You express empathy by sensing the energy of emotions.

Disadvantages

- You may feel tired, anxious, or drained around people.

- You feel exposed or "too open" in the world.

- You are an energy sponge who absorbs others' stress or emotions.

- You tend to get overloaded by the number of intuitions you pick up and don't know how to turn them off.

Finding Balance: Shield Yourself

To be comfortable with intuitive empathy, practice the following protective shielding technique. Think of it as putting on an invisibility cloak that keeps you safe from others' stress or intuitive information overload.

Visualize yourself completely encircled by a shield of shimmering, pure white light. Picture this insulating barrier surrounding your entire body from head to toe about six inches from the skin. It is semipermeable, allowing positive emotions such as hope, happiness, and compassion in but keeping out unwanted stress emanating from outside sources. This option of shielding lets you choose how open you want to be. You can use it just in a specific situation or keep it up all day if you need the protection. Sometimes you also may picture a stronger shield, one composed of solid rock that can keep away people around whom you don't feel safe.

Style 4. Spiritual Empathy: The Mystic

If your primary empathy style is spiritual, you empathize with others through your spirituality. Consider this style "divining empathy," which describes the process of connecting to spirituality (however you define it) to open your heart. For some, spirituality could be God, Goddess, nature, a creative intelligence, or the power of love. The divine is a stepping stone to your large, compassionate self. You become a vessel for Spirit as you give and receive empathy. In some spiritual traditions ego = edging God out, which you are less prone to do. This style reflects the sublime perspective of the Prayer of Saint Francis that says,

> Make me an instrument of your peace. Where there
> is hatred, let me sow love. Where there is despair,
> hope. . . . For it is in giving that we receive.

As an extension of this prayer, you view empathy as a sacred expression of healing that nourishes your soul and the world.

If you have spiritual empathy, you may be drawn to the clergy or charitable nonprofit work. Satisfying careers include being a spiritual psychotherapist, a life coach, an acupuncturist, or a yoga instructor. Or you may be a writer, editor, or publisher who values getting "spiritual" books out to the world. Also, you can bring this empathy style into the corporate culture and leadership models to create a more cooperative, empathic workplace.

Advantages

- You value empathy as a spiritual gift and sacred way of life.

- You are gratified by giving and being of service.

- You practice forgiveness and tolerance.

- You use prayer and meditation as ways to receive intuitive guidance for yourself, others, and for the highest good of all.

Disadvantages

- You may become a martyr and take on other people's suffering.

- You are burdened by the world's weightiness, depression, and pain.

- Your identity is mainly linked to giving to others rather than receiving.

- You may view self-care as an indulgence, not as a necessity to replenish yourself.

To ground yourself in this style of empathy, many Asian spiritual traditions such as Taoism and Buddhism recognize the importance of taking the Middle Path. This means being of heaven and of the earth. It is a way of life that avoids extremes and encourages you to tend to your whole self: mind, body, and spirit.

Finding Balance: Follow the Middle Path

Every day, remember to give to yourself. Helping others is admirable but also honor your physical and emotional needs, your quiet time, and your energy level. As Pierre Teilhard de Chardin said, "We are spiritual beings having a human experience." *Thus, nourishing your human part is vital.* Make time for at least one grounding activity daily such as exercise, gardening, putting your bare feet on the ground (earthing), dancing, listening to music, eating healthy food, yoga . . . whatever makes you happy and strengthens your body.

• ● •

These four empathy styles represent general preferences of how you give and receive but they can be fluid. I want to support you in enhancing your assets and managing the difficulties so you can be more fully you. But I also suggest that you experiment with different styles to keep expanding how you express empathy.

The most significant relationship you'll ever have is with yourself. Knowing your empathy style provides a basic understanding of how to productively express caring and where you are off balance. This information lets you love yourself more and find a comfortable, healing mode of giving and self-care.

The Neuroscience of Empathy

I'm intrigued by the growing number of scientific findings that explain what occurs in your brain and body when you're feeling healthy empathy (not overgiving). For instance, the journal *Neuro-Image* revealed that people with cognitive empathy had increased grey matter (a rich storehouse of neurons that let us function at a high level every day) in the midcingulate cortex, an area associated with decision-making. In contrast, those with emotional empathy had more grey matter in the insula, the center for strong emotions.[3] The brain structure differed for each type. Knowing about neuroscience will help you create a more complete narrative about how empathy functions to heal yourself and others.

The Mirror Neuron System

The mirror neuron system is a specific group of brain cells that are wired for compassion and empathy.[4] They let you mimic other people's emotions and feel what they are feeling so you're in resonance with them. The deeper your connection is with someone, the stronger your caring becomes. Mirror neurons are activated by external forces—when a good friend is in pain, you feel pain too, or when your child is happy, you feel happy. Supersensitive empaths are thought to have hyperactive mirror neurons, whereas psychopaths, sociopaths, and those with narcissistic personality disorder may have underactive mirror neuron systems.

Oxytocin and Other Happiness Hormones

Hormones are chemical messengers that travel from the brain to various parts of the body. When you're feeling empathy, your stress hormones decrease and your feel-good hormones increase to reduce pain, boost immunity and health, and keep you more youthful.

Empathy has been shown to activate the following "happiness hormones":

- **Oxytocin.** This blissful, warm and fuzzy "love hormone" can boost empathy, trust, and connection in your relationships. It is released during childbirth, breastfeeding, sex, kissing, hugging, cuddling, friendships, intimate conversations, and caregiving. It also soothes depression and anxiety. The higher your oxytocin level, the more you want to be loving with yourself and others.[5]

- **Endorphins.** These natural painkillers relieve stress and discomfort. They rise during exercise (a feeling known as the "runner's high"), eating, and sex. Empathic people feel better because their brain is producing endorphins, which brings a rush of positive feelings and tension release.

- **Dopamine.** This hormone is associated with the pleasure response when you experience empathy, when you're of service to someone, or during other enjoyable activities. It can feel good to have your heart go out to another person, and also for others to be empathic with you.

- **Serotonin.** This is your body's natural antidepressant that increases when you experience empathy. It also regulates your mood as well as sleep, appetite, digestion, and memory.

Our behavior influences which hormones we produce. But hormones also influence our behavior. For instance, if you hug a human or animal friend, your oxytocin levels rise, and you feel loving. If you have a fight with a coworker, your stress hormones—cortisol and adrenaline—surge through your system, raising blood pressure and heart rate. So you want to make the most of your happiness hormones by channeling them to enhance your well-being.

The Vagus Nerve and Parasympathetic Nervous System

Your parasympathetic "rest, restore, and digest" nervous system soothes your body, manages stress, promotes healthy digestion, and calms spasms in your gastrointestinal tract. It helps you shed tension by telling your body, *It's okay to relax.*

Your vagus nerve, the longest and one of the body's most influential nerves, controls the parasympathetic nervous system. It connects your brain to your heart, lungs, and digestion (which also accounts for "gut feelings"). Science is now discovering that the gut's microbiome—its good and bad bacteria—may message the brain directly through the vagus nerve, which can affect both your gastrointestinal and mental health.[6] This nerve also regulates your tone of voice and facial expressions, such as frowning or smiling.[7] Without these cues, you'd be hard-pressed to interpret someone's emotions or even know if they are showing empathy.

The vagus nerve is linked to empathy and the instinct for caregiving. In fact, some scientists propose that it has evolved specifically to encourage such caring behavior.[8] Just as muscles can be toned, so can the vagus nerve. Activities that stimulate it (and empathy) include deep and steady breathing, singing, humming, chanting, meditating, gargling, yoga, tai chi, aerobic exercise, getting massages, being with people you like, and laughing.[9]

In addition, any acute exposure to cold quiets the fight-or-flight response associated with anxiety. Cold showers or placing an ice pack on one's chest for fifteen minutes have been used to avert panic attacks. Also training yourself to focus on favorite thoughts such as, *I'm a loving person* or *My garden is especially beautiful today* rather than doom and gloom or "what-if" scenarios, makes your parasympathetic nervous system happy. A "well-toned" vagus nerve is linked to enhanced compassion and gratitude and a desire to help others. In turn, these qualities promote emotional health and resilience.

Sensory Processing Sensitivity

Research indicates that some people, such as emotional empaths, have a highly sensitive brain. This gives them a heightened awareness to subtle stimuli such as light, sound, touch, smell, loud talking, and crowded places. They are also capable of a greater depth of information processing, intuition, emotions, and empathy. This trait is called sensory processing sensitivity (SPS). Because these people react intensely to their environment, their brains and hearts need more time to process events, especially after conflicts or stimulating interactions. People with SPS don't have the usual emotional filters that others have. They tend to absorb others' stress into their own bodies and are prone to sensory overload and fatigue. Seminal research of the SPS trait shows increased responsiveness in the parts of their brains related to awareness, memory, and empathy. SPS is a state of high empathy, as is found in empaths, that doesn't need fixing. Still, people with this trait require coping skills such as boundary setting, meditation, and self-care so that they can enjoy their gifts without getting overwhelmed. Along with this book, *The Empath's Survival Guide* is a foundational resource for learning these coping skills.

The Immune Response

How does empathy work on a biological level to boost your immune system? Research indicates that you can heal faster when your body receives messages such as empathy, kindness, and tolerance. These trigger an initial immune response—then your body's natural healing forces can kick in too.[10]

When you empathize with a friend either in an uplifting or trying situation, your body and theirs release oxytocin and endorphins that strengthen immunity, soothe anxiety, and bring calm. So, when you help someone in small or large ways you typically feel better. This is known as the "helper's high."[11] In contrast, holding on to anger and hatred suppresses immunity by raising stress hormones, which are linked to high blood pressure, heart disease, insomnia, anxiety, and a range of other serious health problems.

Compelling research has also shown that simply observing an act of empathy can improve your immune response. After 132 students at Harvard University watched a video of Mother Teresa caring for children who had been abandoned and people who suffered from leprosy, the antibodies in their saliva markedly increased, a sign of heightened immunity. This finding, known as the "Mother Teresa Effect," is striking.[12] It demonstrates that when you witness an act of empathy, it can create more robust immunity in you. Therefore, your empathy can support other people's health, and their empathy can support yours. This is a powerful testament to the healing ability of empathy.

As you can see, our minds, bodies, and spirits all intimately work together when we express empathy. Your biology is an invaluable ally. Understanding how to tap into its miraculous functions, from the mirror neuron system to your happiness hormones, lets you create an environment for empathy to flourish. Mindfully listening to your body is a way to show kindness toward yourself, others, and the greater world.

Charles Darwin, in his book *The Descent of Man* (published in 1871, over a decade after his *On the Origin of Species*), writes that the survival of the *kindest,* not the fittest, is the most important element in human evolution.[13] He elevates empathy to a crucial survival-oriented trait. Darwin argues that we are a profoundly social and caring species that instinctively helps others in distress. *The Descent of Man* was published shortly before Darwin's death and was the most underread of his books. Still, his scientific turnabout or maturing awareness—however we view Darwin's astute realization—points to the biological advantage of empathy that can potentially preserve humankind.

EMPATHY IN ACTION

Soothe Your Nervous System

When you are feeling or thinking "too much," it's time to prioritize self-care. Practice this exercise to decrease overwhelm as soon as you feel it building. If you are too busy at work to take a break, plan some time to regroup later at home.

Close the door to your office or bedroom for a few minutes. Get in a comfortable position and take some slow deep breaths to relax your body. Inwardly say, *To help me rest and recenter myself, I can pause and activate the peaceful vagus nerve through meditation.* Slowly inhale to a count of six, hold your breath to a count of six, then exhale to a count of six. Repeat the cycle three times. This regenerative breathing calms your nervous system. From a more serene place, you can make wiser choices. Harnessing your biology lets you modulate how much empathy feels good.

3

Cultivating
Self-Empathy

Restoring Yourself
with Kindness

YOU CAN'T IGNORE YOUR own needs and expect to heal yourself. It just won't work.

Like many of my patients, perhaps you've become consumed with problems, frustrations, and duties. I know how easily you can lose track of what is most healing and helps you feel comfortable in your own skin. Instead, day after day, you keep trudging on like a good soldier to get through all your responsibilities—not the most fun way to live. Self-empathy can take the pressure off so that you can be more productive, relax, and appreciate each moment.

Remember, the biggest treasure of all is yourself. Your body, mind, and spirit are grateful for any kindness you might show them. Befriending your emotions from joy to grief to pain, as well as being kind to yourself if you have physical discomfort, is essential for developing self-empathy. The more you apply this skill to your own life and experience the benefits, the more natural it will be to have empathy for others.

I feel so strongly about self-empathy because it is the bedrock of healing in difficult situations. It goes further than ordinary empathy, which is typically more spontaneous and geared toward attuning with other people. I suggest that you make self-empathy a daily priority. Rather than cranking up the pressure the minute you open your eyes each morning with, *I can't possibly handle everything on my schedule!* you can ask, *How can I be kind to myself today?*

Still, self-empathy may be elusive, even for those who highly value and seek it. It is an overlooked area in many otherwise caring people. We've all been told the value of loving—or even just being nice to ourselves—is a profound element in the alchemy of healing. But how do you get there? And once you're there, how do you live in this state more often?

Practice is key. Being caring with yourself must become a habit, not just a fleeting desire. I will show you ways to find self-empathy, a form of love and solace you can continue to draw on when you need them most and also as a daily routine.

We get used to reaching outside ourselves for comfort, but self-empathy is an inside job.

How Can Self-Empathy Be Healing?

Self-empathy is a commitment to being caring rather than shaming or punishing yourself, especially when you have fallen short. We all have room to improve and mature. Maybe your first impulse is to push too hard or get impatient with your progress. Or you may beat yourself up for your insecurities or perceived "faults," mimicking how your family, teachers, or partners treat you. This is a no-win situation. I liken such self-punishment to an autoimmune "dis-ease" where your immune system attacks parts of your body. How you treat yourself affects your health and well-being. Still, even if just a small part of you wants to heal this pattern, you are on the way to enjoying yourself and your life.

For many years, when I was single, my aunt, for whom I have deep affection, would inquire at each holiday dinner, "Dear, are you married yet?"

"No," I'd say in a meek voice, with downcast eyes, feeling ashamed that I wasn't. (In those days, we were less enlightened about the perks of being single and the numerous possibilities for intimate relationships.) My self-esteem felt like a balloon that she'd just popped. Once again, I fell into the unforgiving rabbit hole of feeling "not enough" as a woman. I didn't remember my accomplishments or attractiveness or my acts of friendship, service, or goodwill.

What did it take for me to change this pattern? I was always aware of how shamed I felt by her comment and how I had shamed myself about being single as well. But I didn't want to offend my otherwise caring aunt by bringing it up. I thought, *I can be the bigger person by letting the comment slide* (which wasn't working very well). But with the help of my own psychotherapy I was able to address my tendency to be a people pleaser and downplay my needs. As I learned skills to respectfully set boundaries with others, my sense of self-worth, single or not, became stronger. Once I could catch this pattern and show it more love, I didn't give it the power to take me down.

I set self-empathy into motion by assuring myself, *The woman you are is just fine*, which I didn't totally believe initially but repeated anyway. Still, it was a sign of good faith that I said it at all. Eventually, I was able to accept the intuitive truth of this statement. This let me feel good about myself, single or not. Having empathy for my shame was a proactive step to help heal it.

So each year, when my aunt would ask the dreaded question (yes, I had requested that she not bring up the topic because I felt hurt by it, but she frequently "forgot" and apologized for the slip), I was able to smile and simply change the subject. This was a great victory for me. Sometimes it's difficult for even loving people to change their early programming of certain beliefs, such as what age one should be married by, though they might try. In the case of my aunt, I found that accepting her as she was kept my expectations realistic.

A particularly healing aspect of self-empathy is also appreciating what you have done well. Every day, get in the habit of affirming, *You did a fine job*, without qualifying this statement. You worked hard and sold a painting. You brought dinner to your mother who isn't the easiest person to get along with. You finished a demanding project. You celebrated a colleague's recognition for their work without feeling jealous, or perhaps you felt only a little. Or you were able to authentically express your needs without being a people pleaser—a significant triumph. For example, you were able to say, "I don't feel good about pursuing this business venture, so I'm not able to say yes to it," despite the pressure your colleague was putting on you. Don't gloss over the achievement of empathizing with yourself and others or jump too quickly to solve the next problem. Self-empathy means acknowledging, *I did it!* and feeling good about yourself.

You can develop self-empathy by choosing one doable change to make each day for a week or longer. It's useful to put a reminder in your calendar so this habit becomes part of your daily routine. After a week, you can extend the practice by, say, marking it on your schedule for a month. Maybe self-empathy means staying home and taking a bath in the evening instead of going out to dinner with a friend or socializing. Or being gentler with yourself when you're ill. Or knowing, *I'm not responsible for a relative's terrible behavior when they drink*. No matter the incident, you must be the one to give yourself this gift.

Self-empathy is unconditional. You didn't make the home run or you did. You're in pain or are pain free. You are happy or sad. Either way it's okay. You are on your own side in all circumstances.

Take the following quiz to determine your current level of self-empathy. Use your score as a baseline from which to grow and heal by becoming more loving toward yourself.

What Is Your Self-Empathy Score?

Please answer either T for "true" or F for "false" for the following statements. Your responses should represent how you usually feel. Rarely do any of us have self-empathy all the time.

T / F   I treat myself with as much kindness as I treat others.

T / F   I honor my own needs rather than always putting everyone else first.

T / F   I have self-compassion during hard times, rather than blaming and shaming myself.

T / F   I can set a respectful boundary with unhealthy behavior.

T / F   I give myself permission to be around supportive, positive people.

T / F   I forgive myself when I make a mistake.

T / F   I allow myself to receive other people's caring, help, and love.

T / F   I can be happy with myself when I do things well.

Here's how to interpret the results. If you answered "true" to seven or eight questions, you have a healthy amount of self-empathy. Four to six "trues" indicate a moderate amount of self-empathy. One to three "trues" indicate some self-empathy, but you're ready for more. If you had zero "trues," thanks for your honesty. Perhaps you're new at being good to yourself, but you're about to discover how to do it.

Connecting with Your Heart

The secret to igniting self-empathy is having an open heart. This is the place from which compassion, forgiveness, and kindness arise. Consider your heart "empathy central," a source of infinite love, intelligence, and healing that you can plug into (much like an electric socket). Even when you face seemingly impossible situations or encounter a confusing crossroads in life, your heart will know the way. It's an ally to turn to—but you must initiate contact. Learning to activate your heart provides ongoing access to wise solutions and an energy boost that promotes healing.

In stressful situations, especially if you're about to panic or are in pain, practice putting your hand over your heart to activate empathy. Or you can simply focus your attention on this area in your midchest, which lies a few inches higher than the sternum. Doing this helps ignite your healing energy and break the panic cycle. If I'm experiencing sensory overload when I'm too busy, I immediately place my hand over my heart to calm myself. Parents also gently pat their little one's heart instinctively to relieve their crying infant's distress. Positioning a baby over this area to hear their parent's heartbeat is also reassuring.

There's nothing esoteric about this concept. It's an ancient survival instinct and an expression of caring. Throughout the ages, the hand over the heart gesture has been powerful and universal. Warriors going into battle often use this gesture to convey to comrades, *We are of one purpose.* It also signals pledging allegiance or giving your word of honor. It is associated with the act of praying too. Many of us naturally put our palm over our heart to indicate, *I love you and I am with you*, if someone close is having a hard time or if you won't see each other for a while.

Igniting the "subtle energy" of the heart to heal is a technique that has been used for centuries. Traditional Chinese medicine practitioners call this vital energy "chi." It's "mana" to Hawaiian kahunas, "prana" in Ayurvedic medicine, and "shakti" to Hindu yogic healers. Western medicine is also catching up. The National Institutes of Health are funding new research on subtle energy therapies to help with pain and various illnesses.

I suggest that you also learn to access this energy to cultivate self-empathy. To plug into your power to heal, repeat the following meditation. It is a practical action that you can take wherever you are: at home, in your office, on a park bench, or even in a bathroom at social events. Practicing it will help you feel better and be kinder to yourself and others.

Activating Your Healing Power: Meditation to Connect with Your Heart

Take a few slow deep breaths and relax your mind. Visualize putting your scary or anxious thoughts on a cloud and letting them float away. Then lightly rest your hand over your heart in the middle of your chest, which is the energetic heart center (the physical heart is located more to the left). As you continue taking slow breaths, picture an image that makes you happy: a sunset, a graceful dolphin swimming, a rainbow, a hole-in-one. Gently hold that focus. Feel your heart open and grow warmer as invigorating energy flows through you.

If a specific part of your body is hurting, picture sending love and empathy from your heart to the area. This can relax you and infuse the painful spot with kindness to either jump-start your healing or more easily help you live with some discomfort.

As an extension of this practice, self-empathy also means accepting that you are human and can evolve. Of course, you will make mistakes or have regrets. You may move forward, slip backward, then move ahead again. You are not perfect. None of us are. Thank goodness. Perfection is so boring! I love the Japanese concept of wabi-sabi, which sees imperfections as beautiful and interesting. We are all messy and extraordinary at the same time. Self-empathy starts with being willing to accept your less-than-best qualities as well as your stellar ones.

So, in your process of healing, lovingly change what needs to be changed and be tender to yourself on your journey.

Self-empathy is a living prayer that generates health and well-being. It helps you to grow and heal in positive ways.

Self-Empathy When You're Facing Illness and Pain

Whether you catch a cold, undergo surgery, or experience acute or chronic pain, self-empathy eases your experience. Still, engaging it requires that you begin to release self-loathing and fear. Your body has an innate intelligence. It hears everything you say or think. Many of us are too quick to hate or blame. We turn against our body and treat it as an enemy when it needs empathy instead.

My patient John, an accountant, suffered chronically from irritable bowel syndrome (IBS), though his discomfort level would increase and decrease. Unfortunately, he often got a flare-up of IBS during the stress of tax season. He felt especially miserable for weeks, just when he needed to think clearly. Plus, he was angry at his body for "betraying" him since medication wasn't helping calm the flare-up, nor was it generally effective. I advised him to begin to treat his body as a friend, not an enemy, by telling it, *I'm sorry you are uncomfortable so often and particularly now when your stress is so high. I will take good care of you.*

At first, John didn't like my suggestion. He frowned and said, "It makes me feel weak." I understood how "feeling weak" was a source of shame for him. I simply heard him out while not arguing with his resistance.

Still, in our next session, at his wits' end, he reluctantly but sincerely began putting his hand over his heart and addressing his body more kindly. "I'm sorry you're in pain," he told it out loud. "We've made it through flare-ups before, and we will again." Also, I taught John to breathe out his discomfort instead of clenching his muscles and holding it in. After a few days of this approach, he started feeling less pain—a great motivator to keep showing himself empathy. Because of the partial relief he experienced, he continued using this technique every day, which helped his chronic pain and cramping feel more manageable.

Like John, sometimes chronic pain can't be fully resolved any time soon, or perhaps ever, but self-empathy can help take the edge off of it as you learn to befriend your body.

Be clear about the following beliefs about illness so they don't block self-empathy. Illness is not:

- A punishment or a sign that means you have failed spiritually.

- A reason to hate yourself.

- A reason to be ashamed or to give up.

- Evidence that there is no God.

Let "dis-ease" of all sorts be an invitation to empathize with your body. Remember, a tense mind creates a tense body. The more empathy you have, the more of the "feel good" endorphins your system will generate. These will reduce pain and suffering during an illness.

Whenever you have physical distress you can connect to it with empathy. First, identify the painful place in your body. Take a few deep breaths and relax into it. Connecting with your heart in stressful situations, including medical or dental procedures, reduces stress. Keep sending the uncomfortable area lovingkindness. This part of you—whether it's a bone, an organ, or a tissue—needs your understanding.

Recently, I sprained my sacroiliac joint while working out at the gym. It was painful. As with many injuries, it took time to heal. I was frustrated that I would have to limit my exercise routine. I admit that at first, I did try to push through my symptoms. But to my dismay, I'd get sharp, stabbing sensations that shot down my leg. My body was screaming, *I don't like pushing. Stop!* So, I was forced to reevaluate my approach. Instead of fighting or resenting the injury, I began investigating it. I discovered the positions my hip liked, and which ones worsened the pain. The more I listened, the better I felt. Thankfully, in a few months, my pain resolved. This experience taught me to love myself a little more and show empathy to a part of my body in need.

Though I was fortunate to have a full recovery, I recognize that the healing process may be slower and harder if you have a larger injury that may take longer to heal or that may not heal completely. Still, self-empathy will only help the healing process by loving and respecting your body's experiences.

Healing—whether mental, emotional, or physical—happens on its own timeline. It's futile to fight that. Trying to force recovery too quickly or expecting more than your body is currently capable of makes discomfort worse. Be patient with where you are. It's a sweet triumph when you decide not to beat yourself up and instead focus on the empathic part inside that advises you on how to treat a wound, a pain, a suffering.

Self-empathy helps you learn to honor your body, a physical vehicle that is, really, only on loan to us—our temporary home. As you come to appreciate this, your body's needs seem less like a nuisance, and you'll feel a greater desire to cherish yourself throughout the years. Inevitably, the time will come to say, "Goodbye and thanks" to your old friend, as you're off to explore other grand adventures.

I use the following healing affirmation, which I also recommend to my patients to relieve tension. It is a quick way to access self-empathy and promote healing. Throughout the day, keep repeating it to lessen discomfort or to simply feel good.

I breathe deeply. My body is relaxed. I am moving forward toward wellness and ease.

Self-Empathy When a Loved One Experiences Illness and Pain

Watching those who are close to us suffer may be one of the hardest things we ever do. Perhaps your spouse has chronic fatigue, or a friend is undergoing chemotherapy, or your son got in a car accident and requires surgery. While we typically associate empathy with our response to someone who is struggling, we also need to have empathy for ourselves as caregivers and supporters.

Research on mirror neurons shows that when someone close to us feels pain, our brain centers respond by mimicking it. Your empathy is on overdrive with those you care about. We are all affected when a loved one suffers. It's a human instinct to want to help and to "do something." But during a health crisis or a chronic illness, it's therapeutic to show up for others and yourself in the most centered, productive ways.

What does empathy mean in these situations? Overall, it's having realistic expectations of your role, setting good boundaries, and practicing self-care so you don't burn out. Also, it means staying in the moment rather than fabricating scary future scenarios.

There are big lessons to learn from illness. You can support loved ones the best you can. However, *you can't do the healing for them*—though you may wish you could or even want to bear their pain. And perhaps most difficult of all, is that *you can't control the outcome*. This experience is theirs to go through and learn from. It's not yours to take away from them, though you can lend support. Understanding that this is an expression of self-empathy spares you from getting sucked into a vortex of someone's suffering or trying to control results that can't be controlled.

When my patient Lynn's husband was undergoing months of radiation after an extensive but successful cancer surgery, the situation tested her in many ways. She wanted to be supportive to her beloved—and she was. But as the days wore on, she watched with fear as Jim become thin, pale, and fatigued. She knew he was doing his best (which sounded spectacular to me) with the most upbeat, in-the-now attitude he could muster. But during our sessions, she told me, "I want to stay strong for him, but my heart is breaking as I see him get weaker. I can't stand to watch Jim suffer."

I helped Lynn develop self-empathy so she didn't worsen their suffering. I advised her to practice connecting to her heart every day to access its vast unconditional love. Her needs were important too. For Lynn to be present for Jim, she had to also keep saving herself. This meant being honest with her own struggle. She told me, "Watching Jim suffer is awful. It's okay to admit that, though I still feel a little guilty about it. But to be there for him, I must also stay centered and take care of myself. This will benefit us both. It doesn't mean I love him less."

Lynn took time to be in the woods, listen to the song of the creek, and breathe. She told herself, *I can't get well for Jim or control the outcome, but I can support him. I will keep loving him and myself. I will not let my mind wander to fears of the future. I will also pray to a loving spiritual force to help me.* Lynn's daily self-care routine carried her, sometimes moment-to-moment, through this period.

Gradually, Jim recovered his energy. He has been cancer-free for a few years and is grateful for another miraculous chance at life. Still, both Jim and Lynn understand more deeply the preciousness of life and how with a cancer diagnosis, especially the more serious kinds, the gift of recovery is a day at a time. Buddhists talk about the concept of impermanence, which is the coming and going of all things. Though nothing in life is guaranteed, including permanent remissions, what this couple and all of us can learn from illness is to cherish each other, now and always—and not take loved ones or life for granted.

Jim's health crisis was about both Jim and Lynn's healing. As a physician, life partner, and friend, I understand the impulse to give 200 percent to help loved ones recover. But I also know that if you want to make the experience of being a caretaker easier for you and others, self-empathy is essential. You struggle less when you have mercy on yourself too. This doesn't lessen what you can give. Having empathy for yourself lets you be more present and caring with others.

If a loved one's illness is ongoing, such as chronic fatigue, pain, or illness, it requires us to have incredible stamina and empathy for them and ourselves. A few years after my mother's death, my father was diagnosed with Parkinson's disease. As his only child and primary caretaker (I had no family nearby), I witnessed this honorable, soft-spoken man and caring parent and physician with an astute linear mind cognitively degenerate into dementia and lose his mobility. He required an aid to help him get in and out of a wheelchair and to brush his teeth.

Though I tried to be his sole caretaker for many months (as I maintained an active psychiatric practice and semblance of a personal life), it became clear that I needed help supporting him. So, through a caretaker agency, I found a wonderful, loving couple who was able to be with him in an assisted care facility (which I realize is a blessing that many people aren't able to have). So for over a year, with the help of these caregivers, I had the honor of being at my father's side though this process. Despite his fading cognitive abilities, many times we simply sat with each other, smiling, being father and daughter in those poignant moments that I will never forget.

For me, self-empathy meant acknowledging my exhaustion, anxiety, and fear of losing my father. It also meant crying or sleeping or meditating or talking to a supportive friend. It meant being kind to myself when I felt like I couldn't endure the pain of this experience one more day or when I was short with him. Empathy for myself and empathy for my father's physical and emotional challenges made this passage seem more doable.

Finally, one November night at 3:00 am, I received the inevitable call from the facility that my father had had a cardiac arrest and that he had passed on. Self-empathy also extended to my period of deeply grieving for this man who was so central to my life.

Like me, if you have a loved one who has a chronic or terminal illness, the emotional pain and exhaustion may seem impossible to bear. But if you can summon empathy for yourself, your loved one, and the process, it will help you through with more kindness and ease.

Self-Empathy for Your Own Emotions

We each experience the emotions of fear and love, from which all other emotions arise. Anxiety, depression, and frustration are offshoots of fear, whereas compassion, patience, and hope grow from love. Healing means facing past pain and trauma with as much acceptance as possible. It's also practicing loving detachment where you observe and feel grief or other difficult emotions, but you don't let them define you. No one would choose a traumatic childhood or alcoholic parents, but if that has been your experience, these are your lessons to learn from.

Emotions are teachers, not tormentors. Still, they may feel overwhelming. Self-empathy may mean simply acknowledging, *This is hard. Take it easy on yourself.* Showing kindness will help you keep the faith and overcome fear and other obstacles.

Healing Your Wounded Inner Child

An important step in emotional healing is developing empathy for your wounded inner child. This is the young part of you that felt hurt, unseen, abandoned, unappreciated, or unsafe as a child—a part that is still inside you today. Reclaiming this child is crucial when practicing self-empathy. No matter how tough you appear on the outside, this innocent little being is who you have empathy for. As a more resourceful adult, you must be their advocate and rescuer. Today, assure them, *I will protect you. I won't allow you to be forgotten, dismissed, or hurt again.*

Your inner child was not to blame for your parents' unhappiness. Rather, this precious part of you was not always cared for properly or protected by your parents.

As an empowered adult, you don't want your life to be controlled by your wounded inner child who doesn't have the emotional skills necessary for intimacy or for tolerating frustration. Reclaiming this part of you is central to healing any abuse, neglect, and trauma you may have experienced.[1]

Self-empathy lets you show mercy for what you've been through and release any lingering shame or untrue beliefs from your childhood. To achieve it, you must be willing to realize this indisputable truth: You are worthy of love—from yourself and from others.

To help you get there, I offer this empathy statement from me to you, on behalf of those who could not or would not say, "I'm sorry." Read it as many times as you like for comfort.

I'm Sorry You Were Hurt

I apologize on behalf of everyone who ever hurt you or didn't appreciate your gifts or sensitive nature. I am sorry you were hurt. I am sorry for the times no one was there to comfort or protect you. I admire you. I respect you. Please accept my apology for those who didn't understand you in a heartfelt way. You are a loveable person who deserves to be cherished.

The Positive Role of Tears

Tears are a healthy way to process tension and pain as you heal. They are your body's release valve for sadness, anxiety, anger, grief, and frustration. Don't hold them back. Find a safe setting to allow them to flow. Let your wounded inner child cry. Let your adult cry. Let the overwhelmed part of you cry. Tears can be an expression of self-empathy. Repressing them may lead to depression or a sense of numbness that separates you from the vibrancy of life. Also, you can experience tears of joy, such as when a child is born, or tears of relief when a difficulty has passed. Happy tears are replenishing too.

I am thankful when I cry. It feels cleansing. It's a chance to purge my pent-up emotions or those I may have "caught" from others—an experience empaths know well. Then these emotions won't lodge in my body as stress symptoms such as lingering fatigue or pain.

I've been enthusiastic about crying for years. In fact, during my UCLA psychiatric residency, when supervisors and I watched videos, they'd mention that I'd smile when a patient cried. "That's inappropriate," they'd say. I disagreed then, and I still do. I wasn't smiling because my patients were in pain. I was smiling because they were bravely healing depression or other difficult emotions with tears. I was pleased for their breakthroughs. Thank goodness our bodies have this capacity. I hope you can appreciate the healing power of your tears too.

Crying can make us feel better, even when a problem is unresolved. In addition to lubricating our eyes, removing irritants, and expelling stress hormones, emotional tears heal the heart. Patients sometimes tell me, "I apologize for crying. I was trying hard not to. It makes me feel weak." I know where they're coming from: parents who were uneasy around tears and a culture that tells us that powerful people "in control" don't cry. I reject these beliefs. Powerful men and woman have the strength and self-awareness to cry (though they may prefer privacy, especially at work, unless an environment is supportive). These are the people who impress me.

My vision is that we learn to make room for tears in the workplace. Perhaps we can create or advocate for private spaces where staff can meditate, breathe, cry, or use other strategies I've discussed to soothe their nervous system when they are overwhelmed.

I encourage my patients to cry. It's okay to cry for yourself, for others, or the world. Let your tears flow to purify stress and suffering. Crying is a sign that you're tuned in to yourself. Afterward your breathing and heart rate decrease so you are in a calmer biological and emotional state. Tears are a sign of courage, empathy, and authenticity.

Self-Empathy When a Loved One Experiences Difficult Emotions

If your mate, children, or friends are experiencing emotional pain such as depression, anxiety, or grief, it can feel overwhelming to them and you. It's hard to maintain boundaries because your brain's compassionate mirror neurons keep firing, empathizing with those you love. You hurt when they hurt. Chronic emotional suffering can wear down your resilience. It's fine to ask yourself in these situations, "How can I meet my own emotional needs so I can be of service to a loved one?"

Self-care doesn't make you less compassionate or selfish. It is not your job to take on others' suffering, which doesn't work anyway. You just end up with two people suffering. You can help them most by being a positive presence as they recover. Although a part of you might want to shoulder their pain or feel obliged to, they must do their own healing work.

Observe, Don't Absorb

A principle of self-empathy is to observe a loved one's emotions but not absorb them. Stay in your own emotional lane and don't jump into theirs.

Your loved one's experience is exactly that: their experience. It is not yours! This may be hard to grasp initially. However, if you truly want to help, you must see the person you cherish as separate from you. This protects you from compassion burnout. Allow them to find their own healing path with the support of a therapist, a coach, or other health-care practitioners. If their situation isn't severe or life-threatening, give them time and space to work through the issue on their own, if that's their choice. You are not their therapist, nor is it healthy to try to be.

Emotional and physical healing typically involve some suffering. Tolerating a loved one's discomfort can stretch our hearts, but we must learn to be patient with their aches, pains, and struggles without taking them on. Even so, to be clear: you are not just sitting there doing nothing. Offering your loving presence is a supremely compassionate, healing act from which the other person will benefit.

However, at an early age, some of us were asked to be caregivers for an anxious or depressed relative when it was an inappropriate, untenable role. It's important to understand what happened at that time, identify any emotions you absorbed from them, and have empathy for yourself.

When I was an empathic, quiet, book-loving eleven-year-old, my take-charge physician-mother had a sudden heart attack at forty. For weeks, she would ask me to sit beside her on the bed and hold her hand when she had chest pain. In that suffocating room with the blackout curtains drawn, I wanted to help, but I was scared and overwhelmed. I feared that she might die at any moment. I didn't cry when I sat there. I just felt tense but loved my mother intensely. I dreaded being there, but I dared not leave.

I thought, "I wish my father was here." He was a kind and good man, though he preferred to avoid emotions. And as a busy radiologist, he worked all day and only intervened on the weekends. I longed to have him, or someone, say, "Judith is too young to be here" and help my mother instead. But no one ever came. And I never complained.

I didn't realize that I was absorbing her emotions. Many sensitive children have this protective instinct to relieve a loved one's suffering, but they must learn how to set healthy boundaries. Even after my mother recovered over the next year, for years I unknowingly carried around her anxiety and thought it was mine. Like many people, I didn't realize what was happening or ways to detach from my mother's distress. I felt overly responsible for fixing her, though I didn't know how to accomplish that.

A decade later, in my own psychotherapy, I discovered ways to release my mother's anxiety by first understanding that it wasn't mine and then seeing us as separate and complete people, an ah-ha moment. Such autonomy is necessary to maintain a healthy distance in relationships.

Like me, if you were too young or simply unprepared to handle a loved one's emotional pain, begin to empathize with yourself for being in that position. It wasn't fair, but it can still help you grow. You want to bring understanding to the situation.

We who yearn to heal are alike in this way: we're learning to keep an open heart in the midst of our own or another's strong emotions. We're discovering how to release pain and reach for a freedom that exists beyond all personal wounds. This book's practices will help you become larger than any emotional trial so that you can experience it from a more grounded perspective. To stay centered around people who are expressing intense feelings, say inwardly, *I love _____ but I am a separate person. I can be empathic and supportive without taking on their emotions. I will observe, not absorb.*

Finding empathy for yourself and others is a slow but sure change. As a psychiatrist, I'm aware of how hard all of us can be on ourselves. When things go wrong, you blame yourself. Or maybe you've taken on your parents' judgmental voices or painful emotions, though you swore you'd never be like them. It's all okay.

Despite the traumas, neglect, or pain you might have endured, little by little, you can begin to empathize with your own human plight—and your emergence. The most unfamiliar part may be beginning with yourself. Nevertheless, this is the sacred starting place, the break of day.

The Gift of Self-Empathy: Why It Is Easier to Help Others Than Yourself

Though self-empathy seems like a comfort we all crave, it turns out to be a surprisingly difficult or even alien concept for many people. Often, it is much easier to help others (including strangers) than ourselves. Why isn't self-empathy the first thing on our minds when we need to heal? Why can it be so hard to be nice to ourselves? One patient told me, "I'm so used to caring about everyone else, it didn't occur to me to empathize with myself. It makes me feel selfish."

See if you identify with that or any of these other reasons:

- Most parents don't model or prioritize self-empathy, so we never learned it—though we sure saw plenty of examples of how to be down on ourselves!

- Some people view self-empathy as a weakness, an indulgence, or they feel unworthy of receiving kindness.

- Though helping others can bolster your self-esteem, when you're always giving, you may not address your own needs.

- It may feel too uncomfortable to face your pain or imperfections, let alone empathize with them.

To heal, it's important to examine these untrue judgments that sabotage self-empathy. Avoiding them doesn't work because they are still alive within, blocking the path to love.

We are worthy of the same understanding we offer others. Each day, get into the habit of asking, *How can I treat myself with more kindness and less judgment? How can I be as good a friend to myself as I am to others or my animal companions?*

Be gentle with any resistances or blocks that you might encounter to self-empathy. As you heal, you will remove obstacles, including past traumas or perfectionism, that stop you from loving yourself.

Four Healing Steps to Practice Self-Empathy

The following four steps demonstrate how to bring self-empathy into your daily life. It will help you reprogram unproductive thoughts, elevate your self-talk, and awaken the healing energy of the heart.

Step 1. Speak to Yourself with Kindness

Get in the habit of addressing yourself in a caring, positive tone. The language you use with yourself is important. First, make contact by saying to yourself, *You can depend on me. I want to support you.*

Step 2. Connect to Your Heart

Put your hand over your heart to activate unconditional love and empathy or simply visualize this area and feel the love build. You can also breathe this healing energy directly into an uncomfortable part of your body. Do not try to remove the discomfort. Simply relax and feel the heart's warmth flow to the area in need.

Step 3. Make a General Empathic Statement to Yourself

In stressful situations, you can always say to yourself simple words of comfort to begin the healing process, such as *I'm sorry you have to go through this; hang in there* or *I can see that you're hurting. We will be okay.*

Step 4. Make a Specific Empathic Statement to Yourself

First, identify the difficult situation. Then empathize with your feelings about it and also affirm an inner strength. Here are some examples:

- *I feel crushed by my boyfriend's rejection. I need time to heal, and I know that I am resilient.*

- *I feel invisible around my family. But instead of quietly feeling bad, I will express my views more openly and be nicer to myself, regardless of their opinions.*

- *My life is so good. I feel like I should be happier. But it's okay to feel unhappy sometimes. There's nothing to be ashamed of. I feel better after I decompress. Also, I can reach out for help.*

Every day, we all face hurdles, though you can't always tell by outer appearances. Self-empathy helps you learn to comfort yourself and be your own best friend.

Practicing empathy will continue to lift you out of the suffering of an overactive, critical mind into the comfort of your heart. You can't force empathy. It's a grace that you invite in, pray for, work toward, and have faith in.

The gentle, loving path is the way of the heart. If you are ever confused about what to do in life the answer is always, "Come from your heart." It's a happy day indeed when clarity can take hold, and the ancient admirable values of goodness, kindness, and empathy will guide your actions.

Let my words support you and keep you heading toward empathy. This is not a path to travel quickly. The slower you go, the more patient you can be, and the more empathy can inspire every level of your healing.

EMPATHY IN ACTION

Start the Morning with Kindness and Plan Daily Check-Ins

When you wake up and during the day, take at least a few minutes in your schedule to check in with yourself. Make it playful and fun. Start the day with kindness. Ask yourself, *How are you? Are you happy? Overwhelmed by demands? Anxious about an upcoming meeting? What do you need to feel better?* Then empathize with your situation instead of ignoring it or being critical. Find ways to be nicer to yourself.

Removing Obstacles

Healing Your Emotional Triggers, Traumas, and Fears

ALTHOUGH I HIGHLY VALUE empathy, there were instances in my life when I wanted to be empathic but couldn't. Usually, these were times when I was angry, disappointed, or in too much pain. I experienced this when I was sixteen. My first boyfriend, who had showered me with love letters and attention for two years, suddenly left me for a pretty cheerleader. No explanations. No closure. No goodbyes. He wouldn't even return my calls. As a highly sensitive teenage girl who was desperately in love for the first time, my world was ending. I'd never experienced such agony. Empathy for him? It never even occurred to me.

Two decades later, this man reached out and wanted us to meet. At our tea, he earnestly said, "Judith, I'm so sorry. It was the worst decision I ever made." He even shockingly intimated that perhaps we might renew our relationship. As if I could ever trust him again!

That day I finally got to ask, "Why did you leave me?"

With a sheepish smile he said, "It was a silly reason. I just wanted to be part of the in-crowd," which I definitely had not belonged to. Through time and experience, I'd gained more distance from the pain and understood the shallowness of high school values. I could empathize with his thinking though I didn't respect him for it.

Still, the growth I was able to achieve that day helped me move on from the hurt, even further than I had thought possible. Plus, at our tea, I had the triumphant chance to finally say, "I'm not interested in continuing our relationship or staying in contact," a "no" that empowered me as a woman.

Why would I want to understand his motives? Or try to empathize with him? Isn't an unredeemable action just that: an unredeemable action? Maybe. But the reward of feeling even a semblance of empathy for someone who has hurt you is that it helps *you* release your own hurt. Most of us weren't taught this, and it may seem counterintuitive. But ironically, the same obstacles that had previously stopped me from considering having empathy for his motives had also stopped me from releasing my hurt.

Choosing empathy goes right to the heart of the most glorious and the most difficult interactions you will ever have. It gives you a way out of bitterness—if you want to take it—so you can come from love and above, as the saying goes. Empathy is a true agent of transformation and an enlivening, health-giving power.

However, when I was researching the popular and scientific literature on empathy, I was dismayed by how cerebral most of it seemed, how it was obviously a "good idea," an altruistic quality we should all strive for. But it felt like too much hard work, and, honestly, rather boring. Plus, it's not usually associated with healing, which, for me, is a huge omission. I'm a lifelong student of empathy, but I'm not attracted to the dry and overly academic way it is frequently presented. I know well how much soul empathy has, whether you're on the giving or receiving end, but that vibrant healing potential just wasn't coming through

So, to begin reenvisioning empathy in all its aliveness, consider these common misconceptions and why they aren't true:

- **Empathy takes away your critical thinking, your edge, or your ability to reason.** A well-balanced person can tap into both empathy and reason. You don't lose anything. You gain smarter, commonsense options for how to respond by utilizing your analytic mind and your heart. This will let you see others more clearly.

- **Empathy is a quality limited to "spiritual" people, do-gooders, or sensitive empaths.** There are no such limits. Empathy is a sign of psychological health and caring in us all.

- **Empathy means you become a martyr and exhaust yourself from overgiving.** By setting protective boundaries and practicing consistent self-care, you're not depleted from overgiving. Healthy empathy is nourishing to you and others. You don't accept harmful behavior or betray your own needs. Instead, empathy ignites your heart's healing abilities, which feels great and centers you.

- **Empathy is a weakness that makes you a pushover.** The opposite is true. Healthy empathy doesn't mean saying yes to everything. However, it gives you the courage and compassion to see other people's point of view. Then you can make a strong, clear stand about how to respond.

Can You Have Too Much Empathy?

Empathy only becomes a detriment when giving gets unbalanced. You care so much for others you forget to care for yourself. Or you may overidentify with a person's problems so much that you lose your own identity and sense of self. Also, showing empathy for someone who doesn't want it can feel intrusive and overwhelming to them. It's also harmful to keep empathizing with a person who is abusive and giving them many chances to hurt you. Be discerning about how you express empathy so you can do it in a balanced way.

Common Obstacles to Empathy and How to Overcome Them

Neuroscience research shows that we are motivated by both approach and avoidance when it comes to expressing empathy. Approach is when you show empathy because there are rewards for that behavior. For instance, studies reveal that we are more enthusiastic to show empathy if it strengthens friendships or other social ties, or if people think well of us for having it. On the other hand, it's been shown that we might avoid empathy if we see it as too emotionally or physically taxing or requiring significant time or effort.[1]

Empathy is a natural part of how most people are wired emotionally. When we feel comfortable being empathic, our approach or instincts will be stronger so we will want to express them toward others. However, there are many obstacles that can reduce our comfort level by reinforcing the avoidance pattern—at the cost of our health and relationships. As you read through them, honestly address which obstacles you identify with. It's a breakthrough to admit, *Yes, this is blocking my heart. I want to deal with it.* As always, go gently. Let your change be slow and true, so that you can heal what stops your love from flowing.

1. Empathy Overwhelm

One of the biggest blocks to empathy is a fear of being vulnerable and then overwhelmed. It either seems too painful or unsafe to lovingly explore your own emotions or that you risk getting burned out by other people's problems, dramas, and needs. Intimates or coworkers may ask more from you than you are prepared to give, but you don't want to disappoint them. If you set healthy boundaries such as saying no or specifying, "I am just able to give you this," you may feel guilty or that you're a bad person or fear being rejected.

As an empath, I know how uncomfortable it feels to be deluged by emotions, especially from loved ones. You empathize with them. You care and want to help them or even solve their problems, but it isn't possible. For instance, when one patient watched his mother experience depression, he began to feel depressed, too, until his mother reached out to a therapist and started getting better. Another patient's husband had such intense back pain that my patient also began experiencing it in her body. When developing empathy, this is a predictable challenge that can teach you the importance of setting healthy boundaries and self-care.

In addition, you may feel overwhelmed by friends or coworkers who share too much information about their health, romances, or family conflicts. Someone might ambush you with accounts of stress they've experienced at work or details of a harrowing illness. Your heart goes out to them but listening can be exhausting.

Like me, many sensitive people are prone to absorbing others' emotions or physical symptoms. Too much coming at you too fast leads to the misery of sensory overload. In that state, one exasperated patient said, "How am I supposed to explain to people that I can't be around them because I hear the dryer beeping and the car alarm going off or that everyone is too noisy, and I can feel my toes too much!" They were not exaggerating. To stay centered and prevent sensory overload, I've learned the importance of protecting myself so I don't take on the distress of my patients or anyone else. Also, I try to bow out of a situation and decompress when external stimulation feels too intense.

During medical school at USC, we were warned that we might come down with "Medical Student Syndrome," where doctors in training would occasionally mimic the symptoms of a disease we were studying, which ranged from viruses to heart problems to brain tumors. (Some researchers report it occurs in a whopping 70 percent of medical students.) This is a form of empathy over- whelm, though we didn't know to frame it that way. True, we were suggestable, but also as new, idealistic healers, many of us cared so much and were so immersed in our patients' treatment that our empathy exploded.

No one really discussed how to handle this baffling and some- what disconcerting phenomenon, which I was prone to because of my empathic tendencies to shoulder other people's pain. Also, my overprotective but loving Jewish mother passed down the anxiety-provoking habit of "imagining the worst" about ill- ness such as seeing a simple sneeze as the warning of a dire flu. Unfortunately, as medical students, we never learned to set clear boundaries or address our own fears about disease that could get in the way of helping patients.

Empathy doesn't have an on-off switch where you are either closed down or maxed out, but you can regulate it. When you empathize with someone you can compassionately communicate, "I care about you and this is what I can give right now." You decide how involved you are in a situation.

Just because someone has many needs doesn't mean you have to meet them.

To start taking a more proactive role in how much empathy you give, I suggest that you keep in mind the following "rights." They will help you maintain a healthy mindset and prevent or lessen your overwhelm before it gathers momentum.

Set Boundaries to Prevent Overwhelm

- I have the right to say a loving, positive no or no thank-you.
- I have the right to set limits with how long I listen to people's problems.
- I have the right to rest and not be always available to everyone.
- I have the right to quiet peacefulness in my home and in my heart.

2. Emotional Triggers

If your emotional triggers are set off, empathy will probably be the last thing on your mind. These are your reactive places that become activated by someone's insensitive, angry, or unkind behaviors or comments. Often, when old psychological patterns are triggered, you may either withdraw emotionally or simply feel hurt. Or you may become enraged and respond aggressively but later regret lashing out. You may react so strongly because you feel unseen, judged, or justified in being right. In addition, you could be resisting painful feelings that may have surfaced. For instance, you may get triggered if a coworker says, "That promotion is way out of your league" or your parent declares, "Why should anyone listen to you?" So, you get upset, defensive, and feel disrespected. Also, you may doubt yourself or even feel inferior, as if you'd done something wrong.

When I recently gave an empathy training at a large tech company, one staff member said, "It's difficult for me to be empathic with a coworker because they show up with enormous negativity and judge my ideas before hearing them out."

I knew what they meant. It was a sensitive situation.

Even so, I told the person, "This is a chance to explore why you are so triggered, not just understandably annoyed, by these comments. Then you can begin to heal that trigger. First, try to find some empathy for your coworker. Remember that judgmental people are usually hardest on themselves. You can imagine what's going on in their head when they're alone! This doesn't excuse them, but it will help you see them more compassionately, so you're less reactive to their comments."

It was important for this staff member to examine the past source of this trigger. I told them, "Identify any critical or negative ideas that came from your family or society such as, 'I don't deserve to stand up for myself' or 'It is selfish to set boundaries.'" *These untrue beliefs are based on fear and misconceptions.* We all have emotional triggers that need healing. As you heal them, you won't become as easily triggered or drained by others' behaviors. Try the following exercise.

Heal Your Emotional Triggers

In your journal, identify your top three emotional triggers. Perhaps it's when someone criticizes your appearance or job choice or is dismissive of your ideas or feelings. Then ask yourself, *Who does this remind me of when I was growing up?* Could it be a family member or a teacher? Or a friend who was simply being unfair? Write these down to clarify what sets you off. Then, reassure yourself: *None of these statements are true. I am a loveable, worthy person. I deserve to be heard and valued.*

> *I promise to have empathy for the part of me that feels hurt or unworthy so I can heal.*

Your goal is to become less triggered with time. Why? Because being triggered is exhausting and painful and puts a wedge between you and empathy for yourself and others. You become so preoccupied with managing your hurt feelings that it may not occur to you to empathize with yourself or even those people who have insecurities that manifest as putting others down or making them wrong.

When you honor your true worth, you won't be as reactive. It's liberating to stop giving others the power to bother you that much. You still might understandably be turned off by their comments, but you won't feel as deflated or angry or as if you were punched in the gut. Sometimes it's a leap to reach this place, but once you succeed even a little, you'll be reinforcing a healthier response.

3. Past Trauma

Sometimes old trauma, whether from childhood or later in life, can unknowingly block your empathy today. It may feel too vulnerable, like you'd risk being hurt again if you opened up that much. Early traumas can include being shamed, blamed, bullied, or yelled at by your parents, authority figures, or other kids. Plus, you might have had narcissistic, alcoholic, or emotionally and/or physically abusive parents or mates who wore down your self-esteem, empathy, and dignity through gaslighting[2], punishment, or other manipulations.

Your past can impact you now. Some of my patients who've had early trauma tell me at the beginning of our work, "Every day I live with a constant sense of dread, which isn't usually related to something specific." They become hypervigilant, frequently scanning their environment for potential threats, which doesn't leave much room for trusting others or empathizing with them. Like some of my patients, you too may have flashbacks and an amplified response to conflict when you are exposed to a similar situation. For instance, if your spouse is disapproving or angry, you may become devastated for days.

To heal old traumas, compassionately consider how these events might still be impairing your capacity for empathy and love. You don't want your past to control you. No trauma is insignificant or "too small." Like many trauma survivors, you might have coped by becoming numb, shutting off empathy, or emotionally bypassing certain feelings such as anger or grief because they felt too painful.

For now, ask yourself, *What were my early traumas? Are they stopping me from loving myself or having healthy relationships today?* Then, with supreme kindness, examine whether you are ready to heal in this area. The point of reviewing the past is to learn from it, not to dwell on a traumatic incident or what you "should" have done. It is counterproductive to explore this area prematurely. The time must feel intuitively right for such a recovery to begin.

When you are ready to address a trauma, I encourage you to seek additional support from a therapist, trauma specialist, or spiritual counselor so you don't feel overwhelmed or retraumatized when you explore this tender topic. You don't have to do this kind of intense healing work alone.

A basic tool for healing trauma is self-empathy. Here's an action step to start with.

Have Compassion for Yourself

Lovingly tell yourself, *I will have compassion for everything I've been through. It was not my fault. I didn't do anything wrong. I will have compassion for my adorable inner child who didn't warrant such terrible treatment. I will love and protect them now. I will also have compassion for the caring adult I have become.*

4. Shame of Being Overly Sensitive

Since many sensitive people have been shamed as children and adults about their sensitivities, they may be reluctant to express empathy now. Similarly, parents or teachers might have scolded, "You need to get a thicker skin," "You're too intense," or "You care too much." Or, like many sensitive people, maybe you always felt different and that you don't belong. You don't have to be an empath to be put down for a sensitive nature. Maybe you developed a thick skin because you saw your brother get bullied for being a "wimp." Or you shored yourself up to protect yourself from your father's angry outbursts. There are many reasons why empathy gets mocked or buried.

Like many well-meaning parents, mine made me feel that my sensitivities were something to be ashamed of. I did my best to shut down my openness. If you also were shamed for this innate ability, I want you to know that it is an asset. This book's strategies will help you manage the associated challenges. With this support, you can begin to open your empathy and forge a comfortable relationship with your sensitive self. As it reawakens, your whole being will become more awake too.

Healing Shame

Make a pact with yourself to befriend your sensitivities again. Assure yourself, *I will value my ability to feel deeply about other people, animals, and nature. If I coped with a difficult childhood by shutting down my empathy, I will begin to heal and release that shame so I am completely and forever free of it.*

5. Envy and Jealousy

One of the great joys of empathy is that in sharing other people's success and happiness, you can partake of their uplifting positive energy. When you are able to be happy for a friend or a competitor, without being threatened or feeling diminished, it is truly liberating.

However, jealousy and envy stop the flow of positivity coming to you. Jealousy is a type of insecurity where you fear something will be taken from you. For instance, you're jealous of a coworker's success because you are afraid they will steal your job. On the other hand, envy is wanting what the Joneses have—such as fame, wealth, or a solid marriage—but you don't. All this prevents you from reaping the immense benefits of being happy for others, a vibrant form of empathy and a blessing to all.

Compassionately observe any jealousy and envy in yourself. Journal about what sets them off and note how they prevent you from sharing a friend's good fortune. Then, say inwardly about your insecurities, *I am ready to have these lifted*, a form of prayer. Also, building self-esteem can heal these obstacles to empathy. Your larger self knows that there is enough abundance for all. Comparing your situation to someone else's is like comparing fire and ice. Try the following simple exercise in kindness and gratitude to reprogram your perspective.

Strengthen Your Self-Esteem

Take a few moments to focus on what you've done well and what you are grateful for rather than obsessing about your perceived deficiencies or other people's lives. Set your intention to stay in your own lane rather than succumbing to comparisons. Also, try to empathize with your stresses, unfulfilled dreams, or regrets. The better you feel about yourself, the less envy and jealousy you will have—and the more you can enjoy others' success.

6. Unrealistic Expectations

It's important to have realistic expectations of others rather than just seeing the best in them, as many loving, empathic people tend to do. Idealizing someone or ignoring their limitations is a setup for disappointment. We are all on equal ground. No one is better or less than you. When anyone tells you a fact about themselves such as, "I'm not the most giving person," you must believe them.

My patient Jean, a smart, sensitive advertising executive, met a man who swept her away. "He's so brilliant, affectionate, and fun," she said. He also told her (which she didn't believe) that he was extremely independent and wasn't looking for a committed relationship. This man never deviated from his clear message—but it wasn't what Jean wanted to hear. She thought, *If I'm patient, our love will change his mind.* Alas, it did not. Inevitably, Jean was painfully let down and felt bitter and resentful for a long time.

Making someone into who you want them to be can lead to heartbreak and disappointment. It's like going into a hardware store filled with shelves of cold functional equipment and expecting to get a luscious warm croissant and fresh coffee. It's not going to happen. Still, Jean was hurt and angry; she blamed him for her misery. Months passed before she was able to accept and even empathize with herself for misreading the situation. She admitted how honest he'd been. It was a painful but useful lesson of accepting what is.

Don't let unrealistic expectations set you up for a similar scenario. I understand how much we may want love or success, how we may ignore the red flags that are evident from the start of a relationship or a passion project. So stay clear and strong. Train yourself to see people and situations accurately.

Take a Reality Check

For any new or ongoing relationship, ask yourself:

- Am I seeing the whole person, their positive and negative traits?
- Am I prone to fantasizing and magical thinking?
- Do I believe what people tell me about themselves, or do I make excuses for them?
- Are my expectations realistic?
- Do I acknowledge any warning signs?

Compassionately evaluate your answers to determine where you stand with seeing others clearly. If you answered no to one or more questions, keep watching for how you can better align your expectations with reality.

Don't keep giving your love and loyalty to people who can't return it. Also be careful of expecting more from others than they can give. One definition of insanity is when you keep returning to the same situation but expect different results. Sometimes having empathy means accepting that someone is doing their best (though it might not be great) and subsequently lowering your expectations. This helps you have realistic relationships with more empathy and acceptance for what others can give, even if it is not what you were hoping for.

7. You Don't Like Someone

It's harder to have empathy for people you don't like or get along with or with whom you disagree. Empathy simply means that you can see where they are coming from, no matter how your opinions differ or how off-putting their personality is. I am not referring to people who are abusive here (I'll address this in chapter 8)—just ordinary people who can be irritating or critical or exhibit other challenging behaviors. Remember that we all can be difficult at times. That's the nature of being human. Realizing this can help you go easier on yourself and others.

Liking someone is often a matter of personal preference. In India, when some people greet each other, they may make a small bow and say, "Namaste," which conveys, *I respect the spirit within you*. This doesn't necessarily mean, *I like you*. When you become too adamant about disliking someone, it can become a resentment that mainly hurts you. You end up wasting a lot of energy on disliking people that can be better channeled into happier pursuits. The benefits of empathy can sometimes be more about bringing you peace than changing another person. Even if you don't care for someone's personality or approach to life, you can respect their spirit.

The Namaste Experience

Inwardly practice saying *Namaste* with people who annoy you or whom you don't like. This brings more positivity to an interaction rather than fueling what's negative. Instead of emphasizing whether you like or dislike someone, say inwardly about the person, *I respect your spirit and the difficulties you've experienced. I wish you well.*

8. Fatigue and Pushing Too Hard

When you're well-rested and unpressured, it's easier to feel empathy for others and yourself. Sleep is your friend. It heals you by calming your nervous system, repairing your brain, and refreshing your soul. The saying "Tomorrow is a new day" rings true when you get adequate sleep.

Pushing and rushing can also block empathy. I'm not saying, don't work hard. Just make sure you're not so overscheduled that you feel anxious, exhausted, or short-tempered with others or yourself. It's harder to feel empathy if you are tired or stressed.

Recently, when I was going through a box of childhood mementos, I found my fifth-grade report card where the teacher wrote, "Judi [my nickname then] is a fine student, but she doesn't have to push herself so much!" I've always been a hard worker and loved working, but I've learned to pace myself, so I don't burn out. When I'm pressured or I push too hard (which I've been known to do), I get snippy and less empathic. That's not who I want to be.

Make Sleep and Downtime a Priority

To be your best and most empathic self, reevaluate your schedule so you can create periods when you're not working or managing problems. To meet the very real demands of life, your rest matters. Make a pledge not to sacrifice your sleep and be sure to take a time-out when you need it to repair and reboot your brain, energy, and loving heart. These are ways of showing kindness to yourself and nurturing your capacity for empathy.

9. Toxic Noise

Empathic people are often sound sensitive and have a lower tolerance for noise. When an ambulance passes by, I have to put my hands over my ears because the wail of the siren goes right through my system. Other loud, abrasive noises (particularly if they're ongoing) such as a jackhammer, blasting music, loud incessant talking, or barking dogs can put you on edge so you can't think straight, let alone be empathic. In response, you may unconsciously wall yourself off for protection, becoming defensive or emotionally shut down. You can honor your sensitivity to sound by creating the most tranquil environment possible.

Studies show that noise has harmful physiological effects on our bodies by increasing stress, insomnia, anxiety, hypertension, and heart disease.[3] Because chronic exposure to excessive noise activates the brain's amygdala (the center for emotions such as fear and aggression as well as painful memories), it can spike your stress hormones, which reduces your immunity, makes you irritable, and shrinks your bandwidth for empathy. Strikingly, the World Health Organization recently reported that in Western Europe, excessive noise was linked to three thousand heart disease deaths, and it took years off of millions of people's lives![4]

A sudden loud noise can also trigger post-traumatic stress disorder, or PTSD, and panic attacks. For instance, fireworks or a car backfiring can activate a combat veteran's violent flashback of a massacre during wartime. Or hearing a gunshot can trigger memories of gun violence if someone experienced this growing up. Loud aggressive voices can bring back scenes of your parents violently arguing when you were a child. Loud noise, particularly if it is sudden, overloads your sensory circuits. It can override your psychological defenses so that past traumas, which are ordinarily dormant, surface from your subconscious.

Sensitive people also need more time to process information. Taking a break from solving problems gives you breathing room to make better sense of your life. Many people calm their minds by becoming engrossed in a film or television show. That's okay, but sometimes when you've been exposed to noxious sound, you may just want peace and quiet. Simply resting in a quiet room, meditating, or taking alone time to decompress is helpful. Also listening to meditative music and soothing audiobooks or enjoying inspirational poetry and visual art gives your brain a chance to recover its cognitive clarity, so you feel refreshed and more empathic.

Take a Sound Break to Repair Yourself

Plan periods of quiet to recover from our noisy, fast-paced world. This helps calm your nervous system and your mind, an act of self-empathy.

It's rejuvenating to schedule at least five minutes of quiet or, even better, complete silence for an hour or more where no one can intrude. As I do, hang a Do Not Disturb sign on your office or bedroom door. During this reset period, you've officially escaped from the world. You're free of demands and noxious sounds. You may also get noise canceling earbuds to block out noise.

If too much quiet is unsettling, go for a walk in a local park or a peaceful neighborhood to decompress from excessive sound stimulation. Simply focus on putting one foot in front of the other, which is called mindful walking. Nothing to do. Nothing to be. Move slowly and refrain from talking. If thoughts come, keep refocusing on your breath, each inhalation and exhalation. Just letting life settle will regenerate your body and empathic heart.

Learning to Empathize with Our Differences

Perceived or real differences can present obstacles to empathy. Studies have shown that it may be harder to empathize with experiences that differ from our own. We tend to seek comfort in similarities since we generally know what to expect, rather than in areas where we may differ. If you want to enhance your empathy, be mindful of this conditioning so you can begin to open your heart to others whom you may not initially understand. You also can learn to have empathy for your own uniqueness, needs, and differences.

For example, not everyone cognitively perceives the world in the same way. There is a creative variety of cognitive styles that are expressions of neurodiversity such as autism spectrum disorder (ASD) and attention deficit hyperactivity disorder (ADHD). Each style has its own gifts and challenges.[5] For instance, some people with ASD require residential treatment. Others can operate in the world at a more sophisticated, even genius level (a form of ASD that was previously associated with Asperger's syndrome). Well-known examples of "Aspies" include Steve Jobs of Apple, Elon Musk of Tesla, and Dr. Temple Grandin, beloved autism educator.

In all cases, it's helpful to see neurodiverse colleagues, loved ones, friends, or yourself with empathic eyes. This means honoring various cognitive styles rather than judging them as inferior, though some may pose more practical daily difficulties. The following section provides ways to develop empathy to honor different cognitive styles.

Developing Empathy

The first step to developing empathy for people who differ from you is to meet the person where they are at. For instance, if someone is on the autistic spectrum, you can empathize by being sensitive to their physical or emotional needs, which may vary from your own. You can slow down and connect with their rhythms and pacing rather than expecting them to respond as you do. Speak more slowly. (Or if you are on the spectrum and feel comfortable with someone, you can request that they slow down too.) When you ask a question, wait for the response. Some people on the spectrum may take longer to process and respond to what you are communicating.

Also, be aware that those with ASD are often overstimulated by touch, probing eye contact, noise, and a chaotic environment. As a rule, it's better not to hug unless you confirm with the person that they are at ease with it. Even if someone is unable to verbally communicate, come from your heart and be accepting and curious about them. You're learning about each other. It's an ongoing dance of connection and respect.

I often get asked if empaths and highly sensitive people are also on the spectrum because of their similar tendencies to experience sensory overload. I have found that some empaths have autism but those on the spectrum aren't typically empaths.

I had the honor of speaking with Dr. Temple Grandin, a professor of animal science at Colorado State University, who openly shared her own experiences with ASD. She told me that when she witnesses animals or people being hurt, she feels the hurt, and her empathy immediately clicks into action to help them. She sees her emotions more as "a passing thunderstorm." "I live more in the present," she said. Though people on the spectrum might be less emotionally reactive (not necessarily less empathic), this can be an advantage to help them stay centered in charged situations. It will be interesting to find out what future scientific research discovers about the relationship between empathy and ASD.

• ● •

I hope this section offers a useful starting point to empathize with our differences. Many sacred and complex topics of diversity require our empathy—including the nuances of race, ethnicity, gender, sexuality, neurodiversity, and so much more. While full explorations of these topics are beyond the scope of this book (I encourage you to seek out the excellent resources already available on the rich variety of cognitive functions), empathy can begin to help us understand ourselves and others in these areas, too.

The goal is always to remove obstacles that keep our hearts closed or foster misunderstanding rather than respect, tolerance, and love.

• ● •

As you review these common obstacles to empathy, keep assessing the role they play in your life. This is a gentle, ongoing inquiry. Accept where you are at and aspire to heal any obstacles. In my life, I don't want these blocks to impede my usefulness to others (and they can) or limit the empathy I have for myself and others.

So, I keep engaging in self-reflection, giving myself the benefit of the doubt each time I falter or resist empathy. At those moments—and they will come—I rest and regroup. Then I pick myself up again, dust myself off, and continue moving forward on the healing path.

Surely, we all need as much empathy as possible in our lives. Empathy is a basic life-affirming quality to nurture. I hope you can prioritize it and your own healing. When you encounter obstacles to empathy, pause and be gentle and patient with yourself. Don't force anything. Always show yourself lovingkindness. Love just keeps growing when you hold it close and care for it well.

EMPATHY IN ACTION

Recognizing Progress

Today and every day you can say, *I set my intention to heal whatever blocks me from realizing that I am a valuable, empathic person. I am not perfect. I am gradually exploring and having compassion for my challenges and areas in need of growth. With each new day, I keep healing. My empathy is awakening. I can acknowledge the progress that I've made.*

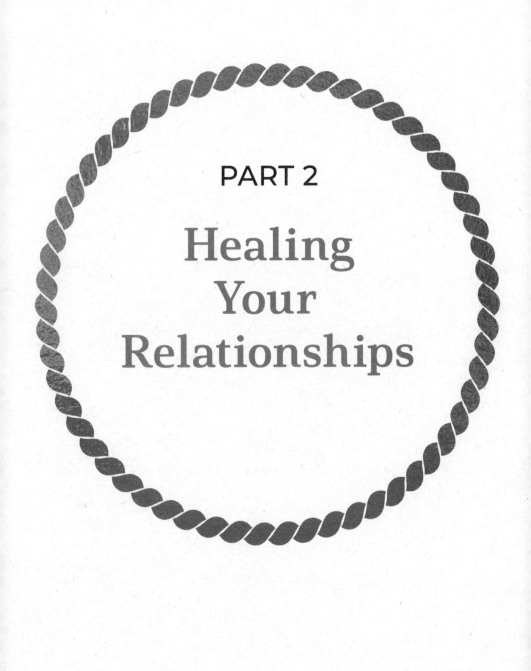

PART 2

Healing Your Relationships

5

The High Art of Empathic Listening

How to Hold a Supportive Space for Others

IT'S AN EXTRAORDINARILY WARM and wonderful feeling when someone really listens to you. You're not fighting for their attention, and they're not argumentative, talking about themselves, or offering unsolicited advice. They're simply being present for you in a generous, accepting, and supportive way.

Empathic listening is an approach to help heal others through the quality of your presence and attention. You consciously give your time, focus, and compassion to someone who needs to be heard. You slow down to be fully in the moment without distractions. No checking messages, being on the internet, watching television, scanning the room, or taking calls. You are quiet. You are attuning. You are present.

I'll show you how to understand what someone says—and what they don't say—with your heart and intuition as well as your mind. You don't need to agree with or even like them. But they will feel heard, and you will gain a more realistic view of where people are coming from. Really grasping someone's perspective reveals new possibilities for relating to each other.

Empathic listening is the secret to effective communication at work, in intimate relationships, and in every area of life. The *Harvard Business Review* reports that the best listeners help support a person's self-esteem and sense of being understood.[1] People, including your spouse, friends, and coworkers, may shut down or get angry when they don't feel listened to or if you tell them how to feel. Then they quietly withdraw or even give up on having a close, trusting relationship with you. That's not the result you are aiming for. The goal is to help someone feel valued, especially when you're discussing a conflict. Oprah Winfrey says, "I've talked to nearly 30,000 people on this television show, and all 30,000 had one thing in common: They all wanted validation. They want to know, 'Do you see me? Do you hear me? Does what I say mean anything to you?'"[2]

Who are the designated listeners in our world? Parents, teachers, healers, spiritual mentors, loving friends, and family members. Let's also not forget our unconditionally loving animal companions whom we may pour our hearts out to if we're hurting or when life doesn't make sense. My soul mate dog, Pipe, faithfully listened to my trials and tribulations during medical school as well as in my romantic life. Animals make extremely caring and rapt listeners.

In addition, you may want to consider (or maybe you know already) that there are otherworldly listeners, whom you may reach out to with your hearts through prayer. Call them angels, the forces of love, your ancestors, Spirit, or God. They listen patiently and offer solace if you let them.

One of my favorite films, *Wings of Desire*, tells the story of angels who oversaw the physical world from the tops of libraries in Berlin. They heard everything people said. As loving protectors, it was their job to listen and to offer comfort. You can call on these kinds of listeners when you need comfort too.

This chapter is devoted to reclaiming this art of empathic listening—so it doesn't become a *lost* art! In our ultracerebral world, which reveres technology and lightning-quick responses, we must be aware of the downside of operating at such speed. Not surprisingly, research indicates that texting and too much screen time can impair our listening skills. The more we rely on these technologies to replace real communication, the less we listen. Our attention span is shorter, we have reduced empathy, and we suffer from information overload.[3] Let's stay aware of this very real risk as we enjoy technology's benefits but also remain mindful about offering others the quality of attention they need and deserve.

My mother, who opened her family practice in 1950 when life was much slower, taught me about empathic listening. As a shy little girl in the sixties, I would go on house calls with her in her white Cadillac convertible. We'd drive down palm-lined Rodeo Drive to the hills of Bel Air. Her worn black bag, bulging with tools—a stethoscope, reflex hammer, and bandages—fascinated me. When no one was watching, I'd play with them in my room and feel their power.

On house calls, I'd sit quietly to the side in awe and watch my mother close her eyes tightly, wrinkle her forehead, and silently listen for the longest time to a patient's heart and lungs. Sometimes she would listen to their stories about themselves, their families, their fears, and their symptoms. Then she'd address their concerns. One thrilling day, she even took me to the hospital to visit her patient—Mick Jagger!—for whom she'd made chicken soup. My mother was my role model. She taught me so much about empathy and being a good doctor.

As a psychiatrist, I am a trained professional listener, an enormously gratifying role for me. For over thirty years, I've honed this empathic skill in my practice and workshops. Sitting across from patients and workshop participants in their rawest, most poignant moments, as well as during times of joy and grace, I've savored their stories, their truths, their struggles, and their determination to heal. When I'm with a patient I set aside my personal self—which includes my problems, upsets, aches, and pains—and I focus 100 percent on them. For that hour, they become my universe. I'm present as if time has stopped and the Now is all we have.

Healing is a sacred endeavor. There's never just the two of us in the room. There's always a divine helper, whom I call a higher power, at these sacred meetings too. With its assistance, I can be my patients' guide and also their listener, but my role is not to fix them. When they suffer or feel confused, I keep shining a light on them and offering direction. It takes time for emotional and physical pain to resolve. I am honored to be present for others during that healing process. Keeping clear boundaries about my role has protected me from absorbing my patients' stress.

Empathic listening is a practice that can be healing for both the giver and receiver, but it's imperative to know our limits and be discerning about how much time and energy we choose to offer. You might wonder, "How can I listen to someone's conflict, pain, or confusion without getting overwhelmed? How long should I listen? How can I learn to intuitively read people so I can hear them more clearly?" We'll explore all these points so you can comfortably incorporate empathic listening into your relationships.

Preparing for Empathic Listening

Most of us aren't trained to listen well, but we can learn. Ernest Hemingway advises in *Across the River and into the Trees*, "When people talk, listen completely. Don't be thinking what you're going to say next."[4]

As you begin to practice empathic listening, simply offer the recipient a supportive, nonjudgmental presence. This honors a fellow human who is going through hard times or who wants to resolve a conflict. Perhaps your spouse didn't feel heard in a discussion about your parents visiting or a coworker feels her contributions to a mutual project aren't being valued. Allowing time to listen to someone gives them space to express themselves. People also enjoy sharing happy moments and breakthroughs: a marriage proposal, a promotion at work, the wonder of a seagull soaring in the sky. Listening to another's happiness is a beautiful service too.

Listening is very different from talking. It is a quiet, *nonverbal* exercise in cultivating presence and showing undivided attention. This is also known as "passive listening," which is different from "active listening" where you ask questions and discuss what the person shared. (I'm fascinated by the fact that the words *silent* and *listen* are composed of the same letters in a different order!) Sir Richard Branson, founder of Virgin Atlantic, says the secret to being a successful leader is to "listen more than you talk."[5] When you're present with openness and empathy, real magic can occur.

I was blessed with having been listened to in this profound way when I was at a crossroads in my life. During the 1980s, I first met my dear friend and mentor Stephan A. Schwartz, a futurist, scholar, and adventurer in a safari vest who has devoted his career to researching higher states of consciousness. Frequently, we'd meet at the same Japanese restaurant in downtown Los Angeles where he graciously listened to my list of fears regarding "coming out" about using intuition with patients. I was worried that it might not be a trustworthy tool, and I was deeply concerned about what my medical peers would think.

Stephan also listened to me describe the shame I'd felt as a child about my intuitive dreams that came true. The dreams upset my parents so much, they told me, "Never mention them in our house again!" For years, I'd quietly suffered, wondering if something was wrong with me. Surprisingly, none of this made Stephan flinch or withdraw as I thought it would.

We'd sit across from one another at the dinner table while I confessed my secrets and fears—and he listened, an incredibly healing experience after years of suppressing my intuitive voice. He never interrupted and even took notes on what I said. He told me, "Judith, I want to remember everything so we can discuss it later. I'll teach you how to use intuition with your patients and beyond." My heart melted. I can't recall when I'd ever felt that quality of unconditional listening.

We can offer this level of presence to each other. The format of empathic listening is simple: one person respectfully expresses themselves about a single issue. The other person listens but doesn't engage the sharer verbally. There is minimal conversation until the end, though it's good to occasionally nod your head, smile warmly, or say a few words such as, "I hear you." Then the person knows you are right there with them, and your mind isn't drifting. When they are finished sharing, if they ask for short feedback or supportive words from you, it's fine to offer this, if it feels comfortable.

Ideally, you can decide on the best time and place to meet when you're both available. However, if there is a crisis that must be attended to right away such as a medical issue or relationship blowup, it isn't always possible to wait. Then you'll need to determine if you have even a few minutes to connect immediately—so you can begin to listen. Later, you can meet again when you're both free. But to be clear: this is not a therapy session or a chance to critique the situation or express where another person has gone wrong. It's primarily an exercise in pristine listening as a form of healthy giving.

To create the proper attitude before and during the interaction, try the following general principles.

Observe the Dos and Don'ts of Empathic Listening

Do

- Create a safe space for someone to express themselves. This is a private atmosphere where someone feels comfortable to express themselves without being judged or interrogated.

- Listen more, talk less, or remain quiet.

- Be tolerant.

- Use a kind tone of voice.

- Come from a place of love and acceptance.

- Show your caring and interest.

- Make gentle eye contact.

Don't

- Try to fix or heal the person's pain.

- Make the conversation about you by sharing similar or worse experiences you've had or heard about.

- Offer unsolicited advice about possible solutions that worked for you or tell someone what to do.

- Interrupt, interject your thoughts, finish their sentences, or talk over someone.

- Correct the person on what they said or how they said it.

- Judge, label, or minimize the situation.

- Fidget, yawn, check your phone, or look bored.

Of all the "don'ts," the one that seems to aggravate people the most is shifting the focus to yourself (the listener) by volunteering too much information about similar experiences you or someone else had such as, "If you think that's bad, listen to what happened to Jane!"

When you relate to a friend's experience, it's tempting to want to share what you've gone through, too, in order to help. However, this exercise isn't the appropriate place to do so. You might say, "I feel for you. Something similar happened to me," and leave it at that. Later, when it is time to respond in more detail, you might ask, "Would it be useful for me to share a similar experience?" and respond accordingly.

While empathically listening, you pause your own thoughts to be present with the other person's energy and words. Make them the center of your world, so you can properly honor them during a time of need.

Ten Steps to Empathic Listening

Holding space is a type of empathic listening practice in which you provide a heartful, supportive, calm presence, but you don't try to solve the other person's problems or remove their distress. In all situations, though, the genius of empathy is that it lets you bypass your judging ego and compassionately listen to someone else's feelings and perspective.

Particularly if the sharer is having a personal conflict with you, the basic ground rules include no blaming, no shaming, no raging, and no attacking. Given these limits, stay open to holding space for them, a stance that is more about "being" than "doing." Your attitude can make all the difference. You listen mainly with the intent to understand, not necessarily to reply. Practicing the ten steps described in the sections below provides a general structure for holding space that can guide you in many circumstances.[6]

Step 1. Stay Neutral, Bear Witness

As a listener, you bear witness to another's distress, confusion (or delights!) rather than getting overly involved or needing to intervene. You are caring, while offering a few supportive smiles, nods, or words. You listen to empathize, not to react or try to correct the situation. One workshop participant told me, "I don't want a solution. I just want to be heard. Usually, I can solve things myself. Mainly, I need to be reassured that I'll be okay and know that a friend is there for me."

As a witness, you're an observer, noticing the person's body language, tone of voice, range of emotions, energy, and goals to "see" them and empathize with their situation. Maintaining a compassionate focus is a healing act in itself.

Step 2. Cultivate Acceptance

Try to be tolerant of ideas that may be different from your own and you haven't been exposed to before or reasoning that makes you uncomfortable. If a friend says, "I won't stop smoking cigarettes even though I have a nasty cough," or "I can keep hating my former boss if I choose to," just listen. You don't need to agree with your friend or condone their position. Sometimes you might learn something new about different traditions and beliefs. Other times you're just gathering information and showing empathy for their suffering, which may manifest as stubbornness or destructive decisions.

Listening is simply that: listening. You are discovering where the person is coming from. Stay as patient and nonreactive as possible. Don't hyperfocus on any comments that annoy you. Take a deep breath and let them pass. Inwardly, you might think, "This person is so off base!" Still, keep returning to your heart.

It's a good general policy to not judge *anyone* until you've walked in their shoes. I'm not saying to accept abuse or violence but listening to someone can help you make an informed decision about how or if you can be supportive. This may mean suggesting that they get professional help. We're all imperfect and mostly doing the best we can. Still, some people have such severe emotional limitations that their "best" is not great. If nothing else, you can aim to feel empathy for (not excuse) whatever caused their hearts to shut down or contribute to their lack of conscience, even when you don't know the specifics. If a person's sharing is respectful, let them express their perspective for the purposes of this listening exercise.

Acceptance is a potent empathic listening tool. One of my friends is a physical therapist who also just completed her doctorate in functional medicine. She wanted to learn new information for her private practice as well as to help heal her own painful migraines. She said, "Some of my fellow students were completely accepting of my healing process, compared to my family who didn't empathize much and thought I needed to 'toughen up and heal faster.' In contrast, my friends listened to me in ways no one ever had. They listened to me and offered much encouragement. It helped me heal my pain even more than all the compelling new academic information I was learning."

When you empathically listen to someone, never underestimate the healing power of feeling accepted. Psychiatrist Karl Menninger says, "Listening is a magnetic and strange thing, a creative force. The friends who listen to us are the ones we move toward. When we are listened to, it creates us, makes us unfold and expand."[7] While holding space for others, stay aware of the therapeutic influence that you can have.

Step 3. Set a Time, Place, and Time Limit

Keep in mind that you don't have to listen to everyone in need, as many caring people tend to do. Choose who you listen to and for how long (say fifteen minutes or whatever feels right) and decide on when and where to meet. Choose a private place where you won't be disturbed. Since open-ended sharing may become too long and exhausting, a defined stopping point is ideal. If the person wants feedback at the end, you can spend five additional minutes. (Remember, this particular exercise is more about listening than responding.)

Here's how this conversation might go:

The sharer: "I want to talk to you about a painful argument I had with a friend."

The listener: "Okay let's set aside a time that's good for us both. How about later at 4:00 pm in my office for twenty minutes?"

The sharer: "Great."

The listener: "Do you want feedback, or shall I just listen?"

Once that's been decided, a structure has been set. Make sure that you're not tired, hungry, or pressured by other commitments so you can be at your best. This structure allows both people to be more centered than in a spontaneous encounter, though you can employ empathic listening then too.

Step 4. Stick to One Topic

Agreeing on a topic keeps you focused. If a sharer tries to cover a list of problems, it can be unproductive and overwhelming for both of you. If they jump from, "I feel my sister doesn't appreciate me" to "My mother has a bad flu" to "I'm angry at my supervisor," it is too much information to cover in a single listening session. If the sharer strays onto other topics, simply smile and add a gentle reminder, "Please, let's stick to one topic." This singular focus will yield the best results.

Step 5. Create a Safe Container

As the sharing begins, show unconditional positive regard for the person you're listening to so they feel comfortable enough to express themselves. Help them feel valued and respected, an experience that many people rarely have but may yearn for. Temporarily, set aside your own problems or distractions. Keep focusing on your breathing to center and relax yourself. Your caring presence will help the sharer feel safe.

Step 6. Pay Attention to the Person's Body Language

As you listen, train yourself to hear what someone says and what they don't say by observing their body language and listening to their tone of voice. Here are some examples:

- Crossing their arms or legs indicates defensiveness or guarding.

- Shrinking into the seat is a possible sign of low self-esteem or fatigue.

- Standing tall typically signifies confidence and energy.

- Talking loudly can sometimes be an attempt to dominate and control.

- Speaking in a soothing tone can indicate being balanced and generally at peace.

- Talking so fast that the words can barely be processed by the listener is a sign of nervousness, tension, or being pressured.

- Communicating in a timid whisper or a monotone may indicate a fear of expressing feelings.

Step 7. Listen to Your Intuition

Listening to your intuition can help you determine a person's inner state. It is a nonverbal way of being empathic and understanding someone. Tune in to your intuition by asking yourself, *What is my gut saying about this person? Is it tied in knots or in pain?* If it is, you're likely sensing their discomfort in your own body. If your gut is relaxed, it's a sign that they are at ease. Notice their subtle energy too. Do they convey a sense of warmth? Anger? Sadness? Fear? Do you feel uplifted or drained while listening? This may reflect their effect on others too. Do their words match their energy? If not, this may indicate a disconnect with their true motives or feelings. Also watch for any "knowings" or images you receive, such as a flash of loneliness or an image of a mountain stream they may be longing to visit. These intuitions help fill in the picture of someone's experience.

Step 8. Practice Loving Detachment

Loving detachment means setting a gracious boundary by establishing a healthy emotional, energetic, and physical distance. It's a bridge, not a wall. It is not isolating or unfeeling. Rather, you step back just enough so you don't overidentify with others' struggles. When they share their anguish about an illness or exhaustion from overwork, you're not ingesting their stress as if it was your own.

With loving detachment, you care about someone without overidentifying with their struggle. Inwardly affirm, *I am a separate person. This is their experience, not mine.*

This skill becomes easier with practice. If the sharer is sad, mad, or frustrated, keep detaching with love. To create an optimal distance, you may prefer sitting a few or more feet away or speaking by phone or on Zoom. In person or online, it's also useful to close your eyes for a moment to visualize the person sitting in the middle of a circle with you on the outside. Both these strategies help you observe their pain or frustrations without becoming them.

Sometimes listening can get emotionally intense if someone sobs or gets visibly anxious. Strong emotions may feel overwhelming if you prefer the logic of cognitive empathy or are prone to sensory overload. Also remember that the qualities that most disturb you about others are often unhealed traits in yourself, and these can be the hardest to detach from. But if you start taking on someone's emotions, use the protection strategies in the next step to help you detach too.

Step 9. Use Conscious Breathing and Shielding as Protection Techniques

While holding space, stay aware of your breath. As many of us do, you may breathe shallowly or tense your body when you're stressed and overwhelmed. So, keep exhaling any discomfort, anger, fear, anxiety, or other emotions you may be experiencing yourself or have taken on from the sharer. This will help you stay centered and relaxed as you listen, even if emotions get strong.

Also, for protection, you can visualize a bubble of golden light surrounding your entire body and extending a few inches beyond it. Picture it as a shield to keep out stress and protect you from overstimulation, though you can still enjoy the heartwarming and insightful parts of the sharing. (You will find additional protection techniques in *The Empath's Survival Guide*.)

Shielding doesn't block your connection with someone. It simply prevents what is uncomfortable or overwhelming from limiting your ability to stay present.

Step 10. Bring the Conversation to a Close

When you're nearing the end of the agreed upon listening time, you can gently remind the sharer, "There are five minutes left before we need to stop." This lets them tie up their thoughts and emotions and ease into concluding the interaction. It's best to adhere to the schedule rather than going into overtime. If you want to continue again at another point, you both can decide that later. For now, this format allows for clear communication and healthy closure.

Feedback Is Optional

Once the sharing is complete, ask the person if they want input (not everyone does). If they do, spend a few minutes offering short, specific feedback such as, "It sounds like you made a great decision." A barrier to empathy is putting pressure on yourself to say the right thing. Take that pressure off. Empathy can just mean acknowledging someone's feelings or having the willingness to understand them. Since many people are used to being judged, criticized, or told what to do, your loving intent will be appreciated.

In this listening exercise, saying less is more. (We will get into longer responses in the next chapter.) It's enough to offer a few kind, supportive words such as, "Thank you for trusting me to share your experience," or "I can appreciate how hard this is for you." You can also clarify, "Let me make sure I understood you accurately. What you're saying is . . ." Then you can confirm that you're on the same page. If you need more time to think about what was shared, it's fine to say, "Let me sit with it. I'll get back to you soon." Never try to force anything.

Also, you could present a concise take on the situation if that's requested. People frequently ask "How do I handle this?" questions. For instance, "How do I handle my father-in-law's frequent criticisms? I've tried talking to him, but he refuses to change."

First, always acknowledge the sharer's feelings. Then offer a short empathic statement. In this case, you could say, "I know it feels terrible to be criticized, but it may be unrealistic to expect him to make big changes if he is so rigid. Even when someone wants to change, it's hard." Stop there. Don't be drawn into your friend's pain. Here, sticking to this boundary will enhance healthy communication.

Learning the high art of empathic listening and holding space will offer you a more caring approach to various people. Keep practicing and experiencing the benefits. Remember it's all about healing. You're generating caring through the clear quality of your attention. Being loving has many manifestations; this is one of them. As you listen, stay aware of that love. Simply let it flow. Being pure in your intent will convey empathy's healing gift.

I'm moved by this passage from Thich Nhat Hanh's book *Call Me by My True Names* about our deep yearning to be listened to.

> I need you to listen to me.
> No one has listened to me,
> including the ones who say they love me.[8]

I never lose sight of what a miracle it is to listen to and communicate well with each other. Biologically, our species has evolved to a point where breakthroughs in empathy are possible once we learn certain listening skills. Just as we listen to the birds, the wind, the ocean, and to the Divine we can listen to each other. I can attune to you, and you to me. So, let's hear with our ears and our hearts on the journey to evolve as empathetic humans.

Hold Space for Someone

Today, listen to someone's struggle or triumph. Relax. Take it easy. Quiet your mind. Be totally present. Do not get overly involved or try to solve their problem. Simply make quality time to hear their experience. You are neutral. You are a witness. You are not judging them or making "constructive" comments. You are extending a loving aura so they can just be. Holding space can be healing for you and another.

6

Practicing Empathy with Family, Friends, and Coworkers (Even If You Don't Like Them)

IT'S HUMAN TO YEARN for connection, acknowledgment, and belonging.

Perhaps you long for just one trusted friend to confide in or a loved one to hold you. You may wish that your siblings would stop fighting so your family can be whole. Or you may want team members at work to simply respect each other's opinions. Identifying the desired change is the first step. But to create happier relationships and heal conflicts with people over time, empathy is crucial.

Expressing empathy in daily activities and at work can be magical and healing. It's a form of rapport you can establish with people you love, and those whom you may not even like.

The genius of empathy is that it lets you keep your heart open and withstand a relationship's inevitable tough spots. It can soothe the roughest edges and the prickliest people. It will also rescue you from the brink of acting in regrettable ways.

Take my patient Kelly. At the start of our couple's therapy session, she was geared up to fight with her husband, Peter. She began chiding him: "You hurt my feelings . . . again. When I discussed my problem at work, you talked over me and cut me off, as usual. I feel disrespected. I keep asking you to listen and let me finish." When Kelly feels hurt or dismissed, she attacks and alienates Peter. She was poised to do it yet again.

Recently, this couple had sought my help because they were drifting apart after ten years of marriage. They wanted to rekindle their love but always ended up blaming each other. Neither partner felt appreciated.

But this time, the interaction went differently. When Kelly raised the work issue, Peter tried to listen and respond sensitively, a skill we'd discussed but he'd resisted. Instead of interrupting, Peter heard her out and then with a reassuring tone said, "Kelly, that sounds difficult. How can I support you?" By trying to honor her needs, he disarmed Kelly. There was no one to fight or blame.

Why could Peter make this shift now? In our individual sessions he had come to realize that he interrupted Kelly when he got anxious. Peter admitted, "I can't stand seeing my wife suffer. I just want to make the problem disappear, but I don't know how." Without realizing it, Kelly's distress had triggered the same awful helplessness he'd experienced watching his father's chronic depression. Unknowingly, Peter interrupted Kelly to push away those excruciating childhood memories. Once he saw this link, he could begin to hear her in the way she needed.

Kelly's big ah-ha was understanding for the first time that Peter's anxiety and pain avoidance was very different from being rude or dismissive. With this new awareness, she felt more compassion for him.

Empathy helped Peter and Kelly to soften their defensiveness and see each other with more heart. Their insights and growing empathy created new ways to heal how they communicated and to love each other.

Reimagining Empathy in Relationships: Repair Versus Rupture

You have a choice about how you approach people. In this amazing corner of space in which humans live, relationships are central to your well-being, but they also present you with the most challenges. Though you may not care for someone's personality, or your values conflict with theirs, you can still treat them with a basic sense of namaste to convey the feeling, *Despite our differences, I respect the spirit within you.*

Why is showing empathy so important? Because you want happy or at least mutually respectful relationships. Because you are choosing compassion and tolerance over drama, ego, or resentment. Because you want to understand those you care about so you don't wound, alienate, or lose these dear ones.

Empathy's role is to nourish and repair relationships rather than rupturing them. It's all too easy to damage a friendship or a marriage. Stop listening or attempting to empathize or keep arguing, attacking, and shaming them—sooner or later, your relationship will either end or turn into a wound mate relationship, which is based on hurting each other. Tending to the cherished people in your life is like tending to a garden. You must support the health of each relationship in this basic way. Finding empathy brings healing into your relationships and helps mend the hurt you might have caused each other.

Put down your emotional weapons and see with your heart.

When considering an overall approach to relationships, clarify your intention. As I have, you can begin by making the following empathy vow (or create one of your own).

> ### Take the Empathy Vow
>
> I will try to find empathy even in difficult circumstances and when I am upset. I will not make loved ones into the enemy.

May this simple vow set the tone for listening and responding to people. It helps stop you from demonizing loved ones because you're a prisoner to damaging emotional patterns. For example, accusing your spouse of "not caring" when they are actually just tired, or assuming that a close friend is rejecting you because she has been holed up in her office for days finishing a project. You imagine the worst rather than seeing reality.

To support healthy relationships, you want to understand another's actual motives rather than your projected fears. It also may be appropriate to compromise or set a healthy boundary with unacceptable behavior. If there is emotional or physical abuse, where the person won't change, you may decide to cut off contact. Do not wait around in abusive relationships if there is no evidence that a person will change, though they may offer empty promises. Even if someone is making gradual changes, it's still okay to leave or take a break until more significant and lasting progress is made. This compassionate, clear-eyed, yet firm attitude can strengthen caring interactions and set limits for unhealthy communication.

Guidelines for Empathic Responses

As we explore various empathic responses to combine with chapter 5's listening skills, be aware that we directly affect each other's well-being. This intriguing form of empathy attunement is called "emotional coregulation." It exists because emotions and neurological signals are transmitted between people, especially loved ones. Your nervous system interacts with another's to support mutual emotional balance, happiness, and health. Empathy helps you coregulate your relationships by mutually improving communication so you're in sync with each other.

What is the difference between listening and responding? Empathic listening is basically a nonverbal act of unconditional positive regard. An empathic response is your chance to comment, guide, or give feedback about the person's situation. Your response can range from simply, "I understand," to brainstorming solutions.

The Three A's of Empathy

Attitude. It's caring to acknowledge, "I hear that you are frustrated and upset."

Attention. Offer your complete attention and say, "Tell me what is going on."

Adjustment. Be assuring and say, "Don't worry. Let's solve this problem together."

As part of showing empathy, it's important to develop an overall policy for responding to others who want support or to resolve conflicts. Along with the three A's, utilize the following guidelines to stay caring and centered.

1. Respond, Don't React or Attack

This empathic practice may go against every reactionary instinct you have just to blow up, to accuse, or to judge someone. The gift of not lashing out is that it spares you and others the harmful emotional fallout.

Even if you don't have control over your first thought, you do have control over your second one. For instance, when you're responding to a relative who says, "You've caused all the problems in our family," your neurochemicals go into fight, flight, or freeze mode. Here's how to counter the adrenaline rush surging through your system.

- **Use positive self-talk.** Tell yourself, *I can handle this. I do not have to get back at this person with anger and blame.*

- **Take a few deep breaths.** Slowly inhaling and exhaling is centering and releases stress.

- **Hold a "worry stone."** These are oval-shaped polished gemstones with a thumb-sized indentation. They are used for relaxation and relief of anxiety. Rubbing them in a stressful situation can be self-soothing.

- **Practice the sacred pause.** Count to ten or take a time out. Do not send any emails or texts or make a call until you are less upset. Sometimes, to break the "react and attack" cycle, physically separate until you both are calmer.

Like many people, perhaps you instinctively attack when you're triggered. Your temper flairs from zero to a thousand in a split second. You're hurt. You're furious. But if your intention is to heal a conflict, don't get stuck in the pattern of, *You caused me pain, so I'll get back at you and stand up for myself.* Instead, simply acknowledging, "I hear you," gives you a better chance of reaching the person, minimizing drama, and getting your needs met.

2. Develop Conscious Speech

Bring awareness to your words. In ancient Taoism there is a sage of true speech, Chunn ti doo yan, to whom we can aspire so our words can heal, not harm.

Similarly, your speech has power, so it's important to be discerning about how you communicate with others. Affirm someone's strengths and joys and resonate with their struggles. Look for what's right, not just what's wrong. Always express yourself in "I" statements instead of blaming, shaming, or leading with "you," such as, "You made me do it." Avoid offering unsolicited advice or arguing. Don't overexplain your position or make the discussion about you. If you feel tired or stressed, it's wiser to wait to raise a conflict until you're more centered.

The following are examples of empathic responses you can practice.

What to Say

- That must have been hard. I know you're doing your best in a difficult situation.

- I'm so happy for you.

- I can only imagine how much courage it took to do that.

- I'm holding you in my heart.

- I'm so sorry for your loss.

What Not to Say

- What's wrong with you? Nobody else feels this way.

- I don't have time for this nonsense. Why on earth did you do that?

- You think that's bad? This is what happened to me . . .

- You'll be fine. Stop being a drama queen.

- Why can't you be like your brother and man up?

3. Use a Calm, Empathic Tone

Words and tone can be peaceful, or they can be weaponized. If a friend confesses, "I've blown my paycheck again on buying expensive clothes," you can respond, "That sounds upsetting. I didn't realize you like to shop so much." Inwardly you may think, "It sounds like they have a spending problem . . ." but don't lead with that unless you're sure they can handle blunt input. When you respond in a caring, even curious tone, your friend won't feel judged and is more likely to open up. But if your tone is disapproving, they will probably go away feeling badly.

When setting boundaries, keep your voice kind but firm. With a friend who wants more than you can give, it's fine to set a clear time limit by saying, "I'm happy to meet for tea for an hour." Or you can decline with kindness by saying, "I'm sorry you're having such a tough time. I'm having a stressful period too. Can we follow up next week?" Your tone makes a huge difference in how a boundary is received. You can say a positive no when you respond with empathy. Practice mastering your tone with easier people and build up to more complicated relationships. Don't start with your mother!

4. Make Comfortable Eye Contact

The eyes are the windows to the soul. Be aware of how you connect with another's eyes.

I've found that many people prefer making ongoing eye contact in conversations. It's a way to connect. One patient told me, "It centers me and makes me feel valued." My partner, who didn't feel listened to as a child, prefers that I keep eye contact when he's sharing feelings or when we're discussing a conflict. As an empath, this isn't always my natural tendency. Often I tune in more deeply for a minute or two with my eyes closed, a habit I've developed listening to patients. Also, growing up, I was sternly told by numerous adults, "Look at me when you talk, young lady!" I felt demeaned and angered by this demand. I rebelled by sulking and being generally uncooperative.

In view of this, my partner and I have compromised. At minimum, I make gentle, loving eye contact in the first few minutes when he shares his feelings and also when I respond. Then I improvise. This has worked for us.

For others, maintaining eye contact may feel overwhelming. Since many highly sensitive people can sense people's subtle energy, their connection isn't solely visual. One patient told me, "It's hard to hold eye contact when I start feeling energy too intensely. I need to avert my gaze." Another said, "When people are sharing deep personal issues, I may look away out of reverence and because I'm thinking and pondering."

Our preferences for eye contact can be very personal and linked to various cognitive and sensory states. If you're communicating with a person who has ASD, they frequently prefer to avoid eye contact and touch. For those who have ADHD, it may be hard to maintain eye contact because they feel distracted. It isn't necessarily a sign they aren't listening.

Eye contact has many nuances. It also might change when interacting with various people. In comfortable situations, it is okay to express your different eye contact preferences, especially if they're out of sync with others in your life. Many cultures have varied expectations around eye contact. You can always ask what form of eye contact someone prefers.

5. Follow the No-Fixing Rule

If you have an open heart, loved ones, coworkers, or even strangers will gravitate toward you to share their life stories and problems. You want to help them. In fact, like many of us, perhaps you were raised believing that being compassionate means absorbing someone's pain. This is not true. A healthy empathic response is allowing someone the dignity of their own path. It's not your job to fix them, nor are you being unkind to let them learn and grow at their own pace.

You can offer support and guidance, but people are responsible for healing themselves.

Sometimes the best empathic response is having confidence in someone. Telling a relative or friend, "I know you can handle this," communicates "I believe in you" rather than sending a message that you must intervene because they're incapable of solving the problem. When trying to rescue others, you risk making them unhealthily dependent and deprive them of the chance to find their own strength.

Remember that tenderness is an expression of empathy. You never know the struggles a person is having. If you just feel like spreading some fairy dust from the St. Frances prayer to create love, not hate, you can transmit your message with tenderness as the Otis Redding song suggests. Be tender with people for no reason other than you can.

How Empathy Heals Family and Friends

Modeling empathy is important in a family. It sends the message, "This is who I am, and this is how I treat others." Infants and children are much like little chicks who imitate and mirror their parents in a powerful biochemical, psychological, and energetic bonding process that may start during fetal development. If you can model empathy, your children and other family members register this and may choose to also engage it.

Pedro, a member of my Facebook Empath Support Community, shared how his father was a role model for empathy. He said, "In Portugal, my father joined the volunteer fire department as a driver and worked there for years. We always had an ambulance parked at our house, which felt good. My parents believed in volunteering, a value which they also taught me."

However, if parents model anger, fear, or anxiety with their children, especially those who have a sensitive nature, the children will imitate these emotions too. Kids who were raised in a home where their parents kept blowing up at them or each other may repeat the pattern with their own families. Still, you don't have to come from an alcoholic or abusive home to suffer from the trauma of being raised in what I call "an empathy deficient household." Even more "minor" incidents in a family can impact you too.

My physician-parents were highly empathic with their patients and, mostly, with each other and me. But they had a habit of picking at each other with a critical, impatient tone. To my dismay, this often started in the car. I'd feel trapped in the back seat as they'd bicker. My mother would jab, "Teddy, you're driving too fast!" or "Turn left, turn right." Worse, she might escalate to express her larger list of grievances such as, "You watch so much TV. And you never listen to me."

My usually mild-mannered father would snap back even louder, "Maxine, you're always complaining. Get off my back!"

I often fantasized about jumping out of the car at a light and walking in peace to our destination. But I didn't. Each time, I just sat there cringing. This left my sensitive self with a fear of being trapped and overwhelmed in relationships where there appears to be no escape. This is a theme I've worked to heal by speaking up and setting limits in relationships, a liberating part of my emotional growth.

Recently, I had a dream in which my partner's deceased father, whom I never had the pleasure to meet, told me, "I'm so happy that you two were willing to get humble." Though I had never thought of humility like that, I loved his father's message because compromise and staying open to each other's needs are ways to be humble.

Still, I imagine how different those torturous car rides with my parents and other similar incidents at home would have been if they just paused to consider, "How can I treat my spouse or daughter more respectfully?" Early family patterns that lacked empathy, either subtly or more obviously, can shape your own reactions in your relationships today.

Finding Empathy During Arguments or Disagreements

The purpose of expressing empathy is to communicate more consciously, to heal conflicts, and to bring you closer to each other. But how do you make loved ones or coworkers feel heard when you're arguing? Let's say your ordinarily caring colleague snaps at you, "Nobody feels this way. Your reactions are weird!" You might feel angry and judged. Still, it's your choice how to respond. If you retaliate with, "You're a cruel person for saying that!" (which you genuinely feel at this point), you'll probably make your colleague more defensive—a lose-lose situation. Why not try something new?

Once you're calmer, revisit the conflict. This time, I suggest leading with a vulnerable "I" statement such as, "It hurts my feelings when I feel judged by you." Then specify a remedy such as, "I'd feel more appreciated and understood if you said, 'Your reactions are hard for me to grasp, but I want to try.'" I'm not advising to walk on eggshells, but sometimes, people don't know what to say to us or how to say it. For them to behave differently it's useful to provide a clearer idea of your needs and what makes you happy.

When I'm overwhelmed, I need to shut out the world to decompress. It's the worst time to raise important issues with others. Sometimes, though, with my partner, I just can't stop myself. Out of my mouth would fly the dreaded, untrue declaration,

"I'm too sensitive to be in a relationship!" Now, thankfully, after ten years, he knows to empathically respond, "It sounds like you need some alone time." So, I take it, and it always works. Still, "I can't be in a relationship" is not the message I want to send. So, in stressful moments, I repeat the following affirmation. It can help you stay on track too.

> ### An Affirmation to Center Yourself During Arguments or Differences of Opinion
>
> I will not blurt out ultimatums, insults, or make important decisions when I'm overwhelmed, tired, or emotionally triggered. I will take a time-out before I react.

What does empathy look like while arguing? It might mean offering a loved one a kinder but more specific response such as, "I can hear you better if you phrase it this way" rather than criticizing or attacking them. For both you and the other person it may mean admitting inwardly or aloud, "My approach is not working, but I'm willing to learn." Or, at least, you can agree to disagree on an issue until there is an opening for a breakthrough.

Sometimes empathy means allowing space for your differences rather than belaboring a point. If you need more time to consider a person's perspective, also communicate that. To register that you heard them, it's okay to use short answers with a supportive tone such as, "I hear you" or "Understood" or "That's fine with me." My partner says, "Roger. Got that." It's okay to avoid lengthier discussions until you are in a clearer, more centered place to revisit the issue.

I see arguments and disagreements as opportunities to find empathy even when I feel under fire. *I don't like arguing—it exhausts me.* But it does come up and has a purpose. In this spirit, always ask yourself the following:

- What can I learn from this conflict?

- What prevents me from showing empathy?

- What triggers me?

- How can I open my heart and let more empathy flow?

Mindfully navigating arguments is part of the path of loving relationships. Empathy lets you communicate consciously and strengthens your bonds with others. Everyone's heart, including your own, needs to be treated tenderly and with respect.

When Someone You Love Is Struggling

Showing empathy for a loved one who is struggling may involve setting healthy boundaries. Empathy doesn't mean supporting all their choices or simply saying, "I know how hard this is for you," though that sentiment may be part of your response.

For instance, what if a family member or friend is experiencing an addiction to substances or recurring depression? If they're willing to get help, it may be easier for you to show empathy for their healing journey. But what if they reject help, as is often true?

Take my patient Marla. Her twenty-two-year-old "baby brother" Kenny, whom she adored and helped raise, had become a heroin addict who also used fentanyl, an opiate one hundred times stronger than morphine. Marla watched helplessly as Kenny's opiate habit continued to destroy him. Many times, Kenny looked sincerely into her eyes and promised to get clean. He never did. Nor was he willing to accept treatment.

Marla and I discussed what having empathy for Kenny meant. For support, she began attending Al-Anon meetings, a twelve-step program for families of those who are dependent on alcohol or other substances. In our sessions, she also learned to show self-empathy and to set boundaries with him.

What does empathy mean when a loved one is struggling? Here are a few examples from Marla and Kenny's situation:

- **Showing compassion.** Marla said to Kenny, "It's painful to watch your opiate addiction destroy you. I love you, but I fear for your life. I am here when you're ready to get help."

- **Practicing tough love.** She grew strong enough to say no to Kenny's requests for money to "make his life easier," a well-meaning but naive approach that had enabled his addiction.

- **Finding empathy for his self-destructive actions.** Marla tried to empathize (not excuse) Kenny's hurt and defiant parts that wanted to numb his pain and confusion. *Empathizing with the same part of yourself that a loved one is struggling with (even if you have it to a lesser degree) softens your judgment.* This is important when you're helping someone out of darkness.

- **Resisting the need to overhelp.** For Marla, not overhelping meant refusing Kenny money or shelter so he could secretly shoot heroin in his bedroom at her home and then deny it. Marla felt guilty for being a "terrible sister," which she came to understand was untrue.

- **Avoiding the temptation to punish.** Marla's boundaries weren't meant to punish Kenny. She was practicing loving detachment by choosing to adore her brother and hold him in her prayers, while also refusing to subsidize his addiction.

- **Letting go of the need to fix him.** Marla kept letting go of her need to fix Kenny (which wasn't within her power anyway). That meant learning to live with this huge unresolved problem—and with her own anger, worry, and pain—while continuing to hold hope that he could heal.

After a few grueling years of accidental overdoses, near-lethal car crashes, and stints in jail, Kenny was finally ready to get help. He completed a residential treatment program and afterward stayed in a sober-living house. Marla is Kenny's greatest supporter. Currently he is an active member of Narcotics Anonymous and has been clean for two years.

However, recovery is always one day at a time since relapse is so common. Also, recovery has its own set of emotional challenges and rewards such as learning to deal with painful feelings in a sober way. Kenny needed to remain aware of the warning signs that lead to relapse, such as when his temper flared or he just wanted to tune the world out with drugs. Both Marla and Kenny understand the ongoing importance of keeping a watchful eye, while also being grateful for the progress he has made.

In heart-wrenching situations, each day empathy may ask something different of you whether a loved one has an active addiction or is in recovery. There are always new ways to love (not enable) a relative or friend who is suffering. Sometimes empathy means saying yes; other times it's no. Or it can mean simply doing the best you can, then letting go of the results.

These principles also apply to loved ones who are making questionable or clearly unwise choices. A relative won't exercise or eat a nutritious diet, although their blood pressure, blood sugar, and cholesterol are in danger zones. Where does this leave you in terms of empathy?

When you are facing a difficult situation where you have little or no control or a limited ability to help someone, hope and prayer are powerful healers. So is showing self-empathy. However, if loved ones are a danger to themselves or others, a more direct intervention is appropriate such as calling 911 or texting 988, which is a twenty-four-hour suicide and crisis hotline.

I was moved by the film *St. Vincent*. The main character, Vince, is an aging, burned-out curmudgeon who helps people in need. Frequently, he visits his cherished wife of thirty years who is a dementia patient in a retirement home. For his wife to feel safe, since she doesn't recognize Vince, he dresses as a doctor in a white coat. Officiously, Vince listens to her heart with a stethoscope, tests her reflexes, then says, "You know what your diagnosis is?"

"What, doctor?" she asks.

He smiles and tells her, "You are beautiful. Definitely very beautiful." She giggles and even for a few brief seconds, remembers who he is, a touching exchange.

A beloved's struggle—whatever it may be—is not only about their healing. It's about yours too. It speaks to what you can learn about empathy for yourself and for them. It's about cracking your heart open, going deeper into love and everything that loving means.

In life, nothing remains the same. So, hang on in times of trouble. A new dawn will come. Stay open to whatever form that takes. Change is inevitable. But until then, remember to stay in the Now. During these periods, perhaps sometimes the only way to connect with empathy is to breathe, simply breathe. Just know that is enough.

To maintain a sense of healthy separateness when a relative or friend is in pain, you can set your intention by repeating the following affirmation.

Set Your Intention

I don't have to have a bad day when someone I love is struggling or worried. I can still have a good day myself.

How Empathy Heals at Work

To make your job and work environment happier, you can train yourself to have empathy for yourself and others too. There are many people with difficult behaviors at work. Examples include bosses who have narcissism or coworkers who cope using frequent complaining or chronic talking. Office politics can be a drag on your energy and patience. Or leaders might not be trained in empathy, so employees feel their needs are unmet.

Still, you can shift negativity at work, whether in person or virtually, by not feeding into difficult behaviors. Here's how:

- Regularly show appreciation for team members.

- Express understanding for someone who's having a bad day.

- Use empathic listening. When talking to a team member, be fully present rather than checking your phone or looking distracted.

Putting these tips into action creates a ripple effect called "positive emotional contagion," which spreads positivity in a workplace and improves everyone's outlook.

What Is Your Empathy Quotient at Work?

Just as intelligence can be measured with an intelligence quotient, or IQ, empathy can be assessed with an empathy quotient, or EQ. Take this quiz to discover yours.

- Are you sensitive to team member's needs?

- Do you listen with your heart, not just your head?

- Can you let others share about a project without interrupting them?

- Can you listen without needing to fix someone's problem?

- Are you able to set healthy boundaries with team members who are draining?

- Are you open to a team member's needs or creative ideas?

- Do you care about the greater good of your business, the world, and the planet?

If you answered yes to six or seven questions you have a high EQ. Responding yes to four or five questions means you have a moderately high EQ, responding yes to two or three questions means you have a moderate EQ, and responding yes to none or one question means you have a lower EQ.

No matter what your score, it's always possible to increase your empathy.

Trusting Team Members

What does empathy look like at work? It means valuing others' perspectives and discussing possible creative solutions to an issue. This conveys that you trust team members and appreciate their feedback. Without trust, it's hard to accomplish greatness as a team.

My patient Eve, a technology supervisor who is a perfectionist, often zeroes in on the mistakes her employees make. For example, when Joe submits his reports, she immediately finds faults in them and brings the mistakes to his attention. Joe, a talented engineer, felt degraded and unappreciated by these critiques. They made him nervous, so he made more errors.

However, since they'd always had a good rapport, Joe gathered his courage and said, "Eve, I don't feel you trust me anymore. You seem concerned about the quality of my work." Eve was surprised. She hadn't realized the impact her nitpicking had on him or that she'd stopped emphasizing what he did well. Joe's honesty was met with Eve's empathy for his position and her willingness to change. In this happy, healing workplace scenario, they could rebuild trust in their relationship.

Trusting your team members is a key to success. You need to have each other's backs. Whenever someone betrays a team's (or an individual's) trust at work, it must be handled with sensitivity and candidness so that the team can work in harmony again. This can be done by sharing the incident with a manager or human resources so they can coordinate a caring response, either to the individuals involved or to the whole team. The manager can do their best to help resolve the issue and clarify ways trust can be reestablished if that is possible.

Honoring Boundaries

At your job, there may be certain limitations to giving and receiving empathy. Take for instance, hugging. It may be your natural response to hug a distraught coworker, but that may be unwelcome or even inappropriate. Not all people feel consoled by hugs. They may consider touch intrusive. If you are a hugger, always confirm with the recipient, "Is a hug okay?" Evaluate the risks of what is now considered "workplace-inappropriate behavior" because of the way hugs and touch have been abused.

Also consider how crying is received in the workplace. As much as I wish the office could be a safe environment to cry, there is a still a dogged belief in many work cultures that strong people don't cry. Your tears could be misinterpreted as weakness or that you can't do your job well. Consequently, some of my patients have decided to cry only behind closed office doors, in the bathroom, or when they take a walk with a supportive friend.

I truly wish the American work culture was more emotionally evolved and able to comfortably hold crying. But there are realistic limits to consider. At your job, be discriminating about whom you share your tears with. If you are upset about how a coworker treated you or simply need a good cry, find the right place to do it. Honestly assess whether your workplace is comfortable with crying. If it is not, an emotionally safer environment would be more suitable.

Strategies for Dealing with Difficult Behaviors at Work

At work and in your personal life, you will often be faced with annoying or frustrating behaviors in others. You might wonder, *How do I apply empathy here?*

With a plan, you'll be ready for such "golden opportunities." If you are tempted to bluntly and impulsively express your feelings to a supervisor or team member about their difficult behavior, realize that there can be unwanted repercussions. It's best to approach the situation in a calm, tactful, solution-oriented way. So keep viewing these people as teachers with whom to practice staying centered and having realistic expectations. Approaching them with anger or irritation will probably not achieve the results you desire.

For your own healing, honestly identify the trait in yourself that most bothers you in others. Is it complaining? Criticizing? Being rigid or bossy? *We're all capable of these reactions.* But once you can admit, *I also have the potential to behave that way*, you're less triggered and better able to smile at someone's shortcomings. I like the expression, "Put the magnifying glass down and pick up the mirror." It is a necessary humility to aim for.

A focus of this book is learning to see people in their fullness. So keep in mind that the following behaviors are simply difficult traits that we or other people sometimes exhibit. They do not represent the full person. To find balance, remember someone's more endearing or helpful traits too.

Common Difficult Traits in People and How to Respond with Empathy

1. **Complaining.** Every time you interact with this person they're whining. They have a "poor me" attitude and say, "Yes . . . but," when you present solutions. They're more interested in complaining than changing.

   Empathy booster. Realize that people who habitually complain may have been raised in a family that talked over each other and never let anyone finish a sentence. Their needs weren't heard. Now, they may overcompensate by complaining since they didn't have a role model for resolving conflicts.

   Empathic response. Set clear boundaries. Limit the time you spend discussing complaints. For instance, warmly tell a coworker, "I can see how much stress this is causing you. I'll hold positive thoughts for a speedy resolution. I am on a deadline for this project now. When things quiet down for me and you're ready to explore solutions, let's find a time," or else refer them to human resources to help resolve a work issue.

2. **Inspecting and correcting.** This person often tells you what to do and offers unsolicited advice, which alienates you. They keep correcting you with "better" ways to handle your boss or your job or even to cook dinner. They feel it's their duty to point out flaws so you can "improve."

   Empathy booster. Realize that their parents likely had behavior that could be controlling or suffocating, or they were in the habit of finding fault. Since children model their parents, as adults they often show similar tendencies to control and correct others too.

Empathic response. In a relaxed, caring tone, say to the coworker, "I value your opinion and will consider it. I need more time to think this through." Tell a team member, "I appreciate your feedback; many thanks." You are not apologizing or appeasing them. You simply recognize their input so they feel heard. Later, assess if there is any truth to their perspective, while doing what feels intuitively best to you.

3. **Chronic talking.** At first, this person might seem interesting, but when the talking never ends, you feel tired. You wait for an opening to get a word in, but it doesn't come. Or they might physically move in so close they're practically breathing on you. You edge backward, but they step closer again. One patient said about such a coworker, "Whenever I spot this person my colon goes into spasm."

   Empathy booster. They were likely raised in a family that pushed away uncomfortable feelings by overtalking. Ongoing chattering was a defense to block painful emotions or deeper issues.

   Empathic response. These people don't respond to nonverbal cues, so you must interrupt, as awkward as that might feel. To exit the conversation, you can say nicely, "I apologize for interrupting, but I'm late for another commitment," or "Please excuse me, I have to go to the restroom." Or listen to a coworker for a few minutes then express in a neutral tone, "I'd like to contribute to the discussion too." If you convey your needs succinctly and matter-of-factly without irritation, you can be better heard.

4. **Passive aggressive**. This person expresses anger with a smile. They tend to make excuses and dodge being accountable for their behavior. For instance, a coworker promises to help you with a project that needs to be turned in, but they don't come through and unapologetically say with a smile, "I had too many commitments. It wasn't on my list of priorities." Or a colleague might "accidentally" overlook inviting you to a meeting that would move your work forward. At minimum, these incidents are red flags that someone might not be dependable. Still, people with passive-aggressive behavior tend to repeat the pattern, so stay aware. These people can leave you feeling bad and devalued but are "nice" about it.

   Empathy booster. Consider that their indirect jabs and excuses could have been the only ways to safely express anger toward punitive parents. Also, these may have been coping mechanisms to gain control in their family or dodge stressful situations.

   Empathic response. Be precise about what you want them to do. For instance, "It's important that you come through when you commit to a project or when you include me in a meeting." Though they still might try to slip through a loophole, if you remain direct and don't blame them, they're more likely to meet your needs.

Empathy is invaluable when responding to others at work and in the world. It lets you be caring while staying centered, so they are more apt to meet your needs.

• ● •

The coolest, most together people I know are the ones who exemplify everyday empathy. They are regular humans, doing their best, but who aren't "perfect." A loved one's happiness is important to them. A coworker's needs are valued. They don't brag or get a charge out of putting people down to build themselves up. They aspire to be simple and humble. Even when their lives are messy, they find something to be grateful for. *An empathic life isn't about being perfect.* It is magnificently and unapologetically human as it evolves toward the good.

Empathy, attunement, rapport, compassion: keep these attributes in mind in your relationships and throughout your life. Doing your best to achieve them is enough. Little by little, growth can happen if you remain open to it. I love this simple, profound passage from the *Tao Te Ching*:

> The gentlest thing in the world
> overcomes the hardest thing in the world.[1]

Use this chapter's techniques to show empathy in ways that feel authentic. If you can't reach it now, that's fine. Empathy is never about forcing anything or going too fast. Rather, in relationships, you may need to retreat and regroup before you act. I prefer going slowly like a turtle. Doing this instills poise and power, especially when your adrenaline is surging. So be patient with yourself and with others.

As you bring empathy into your relationships, always consult your heart as well as reason. With some people you'll be kind but firm. With others, you will be fluid and yielding. When someone can't or won't change—and their pluses outweigh their minuses—empathy means appreciating their positive aspects and practicing tolerance for everything else. With difficult people, this balanced approach will bring more harmony, healing, and happiness into a variety of interactions.

Set Gracious Boundaries

Practice saying a loving, empathic "No" or "Not now" in a work relationship that could benefit from setting a new healthy boundary. Be tactful yet clear about what you're asking. Approach the person with a generosity of spirit while also expressing your needs.

7

Healthy Giving

Caring Without Being a Martyr, Overhelping, or Burning Out

GIVING TO OTHERS IN need and to yourself when you're hurting is a kind, generous, healing impulse. Still, like many of my patients, you might wonder, "How can I be a giving person without burning out? How can I be compassionate without absorbing others' stress?

Being of service lets you put empathy into action. I will show you how this applies to both giving and receiving so you don't risk the very real compassion fatigue and exhaustion that can come from being a super-giver or from overhelping. A mindful approach to energy in and energy out will protect your well-being, support your immune system, and improve the quality of your relationships.

Giving is beautiful, but I've known many people who sacrificed the last molecule of their being trying to help someone who may not even have wanted their help. Or they exhaust themselves by trying to fix others. So to maximize how your giving can heal others and yourself, you need to learn to remain discerning and balanced.

The desire to give flows naturally from having empathy. You care. You want to help. So you offer your time, your knowledge, and your energy. (For me, time is my most valuable gift.) Perhaps you listen to a coworker who is going through a tough divorce, or you do a load of wash for an ailing neighbor. Maybe you simply smile at a stranger.

You can also give by helping others shine. Just as you empathize with people's sadness, you can also resonate with their dreams. This can mean believing in your daughter's passion to become a journalist when she doubts herself, spreading the word about a colleague's work, or sharing a friend's delight about a trip to Hawaii. Being an angel for others and cheering on their happiness and success can uplift you too.

We need loyal allies in our overwhelming, me-first world where so many people feel chronically lonely and empathy deprived. Having even one ally is a blessing. Similarly, helping each other shine nurtures us as individuals and a community.

To all my allies I say:

Your belief in me raises my spirit higher.

Your empathy makes me feel cared for and understood.

Your generosity makes me feel valued.

Showing empathy for others is a powerful form of giving. I am inspired by the 14th Dalai Lama's prayer about helping others in the book *Ethics for the New Millennium* in which he seeks to be "a guide for those who have lost their way" and "a bridge for those with rivers to cross."[1] In our own unique styles, we can do this too.

This chapter will cover the link between empathy and giving as well as how to maintain your sanity, caring, and energy when you are caregiving. We'll examine the neuroscience behind the "giver's glow" and "helper's high" and how to avoid empathy fatigue.

Healthy Giving

It's a myth that healthy giving is only unconditional or selfless. Healthy giving may also be conditional. Healthy giving comes from your heart but is also about setting boundaries in situations that warrant it and practicing self-care. One form of giving is showing someone appreciation, whether it's for taking out the trash, filling in for you at work, or writing a moving novel. Appreciation helps people feel validated and to flourish. It can lift you out of a miserable mood so you can think, "Maybe this situation isn't so bad after all." You may give just for the joy of it, without expectations, or you may have implicit or explicit built-in agreements in your relationships such as, *I'll always be generous with my kids* or *My friends and I will be emotionally there for each other* or *At work, we all back each other up.*

I teach my patients how to give wisely, sometimes a life-or-death concern. It's a lesson in balance and conserving energy that many of us overly nice people need to learn. You'll learn to empathize without sacrificing your own well-being. Here are some positive traits of a giver.

Traits of a Healthy Giver

- Empathizes without feeling drained
- Practices random acts of kindness
- Sets healthy boundaries such as saying a positive no
- Prioritizes self-care, rest, and alone time to replenish their energy
- Feels nourished by giving
- Knows their own limits
- Accepts support

- Delegates responsibilities
- Allows others the dignity of their own path without interfering

Gradually, you can incorporate many of these traits into your life. Learning to balance empathy with self-care is an ongoing healing process.

The Neuroscience of Healthy Giving

Neuroscience has confirmed numerous ways that healthy giving enhances wellness.[2] For instance, volunteering has been shown to lower stress levels, reduce depression, and lessen your aches and pains.[3] Plus, fMRI scans have demonstrated that donating to a worthy cause increases dopamine, the pleasure hormone.[4] Contributing to a community also has been proven to enhance people's ability to cope with addiction and bereavement.

The Happiness Trifecta

I am particularly intrigued by what brain researchers refer to as the happiness trifecta, a biochemical mood-elevating response that you experience by helping others.[5] Here's how it works: Giving stimulates three potent neurotransmitters that drive your health and mood: oxytocin (the love hormone), serotonin (the happiness hormone), and dopamine (the pleasure hormone mentioned above). It creates a rush of happiness in your body while also lowering cortisol, the stress hormone. This, along with the "feel good" endorphins, accounts for the giver's glow and helper's high.[6] The practical implications are exciting. If you are having a bad day, giving helps you harness your biology to buffer stress and create optimism and well-being.

I'm also heartened by research reported in the journal *Psychosomatic Medicine*, which compares the biological benefits of giving and receiving. In the study, participants were asked about times when they either gave or received help. Their responses were measured in a series of neuroimaging tests. The study found that giving reduced stress and lit up the brain's reward centers more than receiving. This suggests that our brains are hardwired to feel better from giving and are less rewarded by selfishness, truly good news for our species's future.[7]

Empathy fuels your desire to give and giving fuels your brain, cells, and quality of life. I commend futurist Jason Silva's idea that we adopt a new definition of a billionaire, which is, "Will you positively touch a billion people?"[8] Imagine all the love and stress relief that a billion acts of giving could generate. That's the kind of world I want to live in.

Anonymous Giving: Random Acts of Kindness

To create more empathy and generosity in daily life, practicing random acts of kindness and anonymous giving are fun forms of service. You give just for you and the recipient of your goodwill.

Random acts of kindness include helping an elder across the street or holding the elevator door open for a mother with young kids. When I do these simple things, it makes people happy, and perhaps even offers them a glimmer of hope for our harried world. For example, I adore letting people go ahead of me in a long, slow-moving line at the market. Something magical happens when I offer, "Would you like to go before me?" The recipient's eyes suddenly light up. They become friendlier. We have a short burst of genuine connection. "That's so nice of you," they exclaim with a smile. Amid the stressors of life, our brief interaction made the day brighter for both of us and added more positivity in the world.

When you give anonymously, you give without seeking credit or acknowledgment. No one knows your name. Over the years, I've secretly left small amounts of money for people to discover.

I'll put five dollars on a shelf in a store or ten dollars in a planter in an office building. Typically, when people find money, they see it as an auspicious "sign." I am thrilled that such a small gesture can uplift someone's attitude. Try it! Enjoy all the good energy anonymous giving creates.

Being of service gets you out of your head and into your heart. Ironically, I've found that this strategy also works especially well if I'm frustrated or depressed, and I don't feel like giving at all. Even so, when I talk myself into being of service to someone, anyone, it has always lightened my mood.

People are starving for empathy and civility, even if on the surface they appear as if they don't care. They may be so rushed or tightly scheduled they don't have time to do something kind for a stranger. But I hope you will. It lets you feel the healing surge of giving in the most ordinary circumstances.

When People Ask for Help

It's a very special circumstance when someone asks for help. Instead of you offering unsolicited advice, which usually isn't received well, they give you an opening to assist them. But, still, you might wonder, *How much do I give or say? How honest shall I be?*

To determine this, you can frankly inquire, "Would you like me to be direct?" I usually err on the side of saying less, not more. My intent is not to alarm someone, but to be helpful. Over the years, I've learned that when people ask, "Judith, what does your intuition say about ___?" they mostly want good news. So, I factor that awareness into any request and use my read of the person to offer the most empathic and useful response.

For instance, my friend Ellie asked me for feedback on a letter she was about to send to her new publisher, airing her many complaints about how they treated her recent first book launch. Reviewing it, I thought, *Oh, no.* It was filled with her uncensored rage and blame about them "not doing enough."

I didn't want to offend my friend. I also knew she would be hurting herself and the book if she sent that letter. So, I asked Ellie, "Shall I be honest?"

Without hesitation, she responded, "Absolutely."

First, I empathized with all the landmines one typically encounters when releasing a first book since most new authors aren't savvy about the publishing process. Then I said without judging, "Ellie, you've written a healthy rage letter. It's great that you got your feelings out. Still, sending it will alienate the people you need to be on your side. Instead, here is the tone I suggest." So, I sent Ellie an example of how to thank her publishing team for their help and enlist their goodwill moving forward. She could do this by acknowledging the hard work team members had put into the book and showing appreciation for what was done well. Going forward, she could start a correspondence with, "It would be great if . . ." then specify the change she'd like to improve the process, rather than, "You're not doing enough. I'm upset that we're not selling more books!" Ellie accepted my advice and applied it, which isn't always the case. Fortunately, it was effective.

When people ask for direct help, always lead with empathy for at least some of their position, even if you disagree with the rest. Then, with a caring tone, you can address the harder part of what they're asking. When you offer tough love advice with respect and empathy, you can be more easily heard.

Be gentle with yourself as you learn different ways to express empathy. It's fine to be discriminating in how you choose to give. With some people you may give a lot, with others a little or none at all. You must trust your intuition and modify your approach according to the circumstances.

Codependent Giving

Codependency can be defined as a relationship that has become so unhealthily enmeshed that people lose their individual strength and power. Typically, a person with codependent traits feels overly responsible for others and picks up the slack in relationships and at work. They want everyone to be happy. So they go overboard and become people pleasers and peacemakers in their relationships. They have difficulty asserting their own needs for fear of rejection or disapproval. There's a joke that when a codependent dies, it is your life that passes before their eyes.

If you're a codependent giver, it can be difficult to step back and let others learn from their mistakes. Though you mean well, you want to overhelp or fix people or believe that you are needed to intervene. You might have learned this habit from living with someone who is struggling with drinking or who has narcissism or experiences anxiety.

Many caring people have codependent tendencies, but not all codependent givers are empaths. Codependency is more an instinct to overgive and caretake than an indicator of how much empathy someone has. You can be a codependent without being an empath. Empaths absorb the stress and symptoms of others, not something all codependents do. Commonly, though, both may have trouble setting boundaries and seeing others as separate. Their healing involves learning to be attentive listeners without feeling that it is their job to take on others' problems.

In contrast to healthy giving, codependent giving often means caring more about others than yourself. Though you may be well-intentioned and genuinely want to help, you tend to neglect your own needs and overgive to the point of exhaustion, even to people who treat you poorly. You may risk becoming a martyr.

In fact, giving isn't always beneficial to the giver. I've seen how codependent giving can take a huge physical and emotional toll on my patients. It leaves people feeling drained and unappreciated. Giving is supposed to feel good. If it doesn't, something is off.

> **In healthy relationships, you don't have to work
> so hard emotionally all the time.**

Is Your Giving Reciprocated?

A common dilemma that many people who are codependent givers face is, *Do I show up for friends or relatives if they don't show up for me?*

Diana, a workshop participant in her forties who had a heart of gold, was in that situation. She told the group, "I empathize with my friends' problems. I'm happy to help. I want them to feel supported. But when I get sick or injured, no one is there for me! It's hard enough to ask for help but when I do, my friends still don't show up. Later they come back wanting advice and support again. It feels terrible."

Like many codependents, Diana's giving only went one direction—out. Admitting this to herself and the group touched a vulnerable spot inside her. Diana honestly revealed that she felt unworthy of equal friendships and that she needed to earn people's love. She also feared being rejected if she asserted her needs.

Overgiving and abandonment are connected. The unconscious motive is, "If I keep giving, people won't leave me." Also, growing up in a charitable and conservative religious home, Diana was taught that compassionate people always give unconditionally, whereas selfish people set boundaries and practice self-care. These programmed beliefs kept her stuck in relationship patterns that Diana was finally ready to heal.

So, on that sunny August day in our workshop, she was willing to consider another narrative—that she, too, deserved the love she kept showering on others and that didn't make her selfish. So, I advised, "In a kind, nonblaming tone, begin to raise this subject with friends. Start with the easiest ones. Tell them how much you value mutual support. See if they want to reciprocate.

If so, great. If not, or if they just offer lip service with no follow-through, perhaps consider being less available to them."

Following the workshop, Diana courageously began to raise this issue with friends. She stumbled and felt nervous but did it! A month later, she wrote me that most people were happy to support her too. A friend said, "I was so used to you giving that I blanked out on also supporting you since you never asked for it!" Only one person became defensive and called her "self-absorbed." This information was a good reality check. In the end, she chose relationships where the support was mutual.

Now, evaluate your mode of giving using the traits below so that being of service to others can feel more balanced and gratifying.

Traits of a Codependent Giver

- I put others' needs above my own.
- I keep giving to people who don't return my caring.
- I feel exhausted from overhelping or being a martyr.
- I am a people pleaser—working overtime to make others happy.
- I feel guilty saying no or asking for help.
- I can be overcontrolling and micromanage others' lives or offer unsolicited advice.
- I fear rejection or abandonment if I express my needs.
- I try to rescue people from their problems.
- I believe it is my job to take on the suffering of others and the world.
- I can smother people with my generosity.

The more traits you identify with, the higher your tendency is to be a codependent giver and experience empathy overload. Having even one trait suggests some codependency is present. Be gentle with yourself. Begin to balance how much you give and receive. Your goal is to express empathy in a balanced way and feel good.

The Martyr Complex

The martyr complex, or feeling compelled to self-sacrifice even if it harms you, is recognized by mental health professionals. It is a particularly dangerous form of codependency. Showing empathy is one thing, but shouldering others' problems can have disastrous consequences.

Over the years, numerous patients have come to me exhausted, depressed, or with chronic pain and autoimmune disorders. Most were extremely caring individuals. However, they believed that their duty as compassionate people was to give without limits or concern for their own welfare. Or they sacrificed their energy to avoid conflict. So they became the designated peacemakers or martyrs. As a result, their bodies and spirits suffered.

Frequent beliefs held by martyrs are *I need to put up with my family's insults because they don't know better* and *I'm sacrificing my time and energy just to help you.* A martyr may feel stuck in a thankless job, but they stay and suffer. They often make others feel guilty for doing too little, which is frustrating to deal with.

Being a martyr has no appeal for me. I want longevity in my work; I don't want to burn out as so many healers with martyr tendencies often do. A lesson to keep learning is that healers and empathic people can be compassionate without taking on others' problems and pain at the risk of their own health.

Whenever I catch myself feeling overly responsible for someone and working too hard to help them, I call on this commonsense guidance from Al-Anon:

I didn't cause it.

I can't control it.

And I can't cure it.[9]

Remind yourself of these "three Cs" when you are tempted to go overboard with self-sacrifice. Having a martyr complex is not a well-balanced use of empathy. I'd like you to explore the many more energizing possibilities for giving that I present.

Giving Versus Enabling

Sometimes giving may not be in the form that you had expected. One weekend I visited two wonderfully eccentric and caring artist friends on the wild Oregon coast who were both also unapologetic chain-smokers and alcoholics.

I was so thrilled to see them, I underestimated the impact their smoking and drinking would have on me. *I can surely tolerate it for a few days*, I thought. But after only a few hours, my eyes stung, my lungs were irritated, and my clothes reeked of smoke. And there was no escape from the stench of Scotch permeating the indoor air.

As a houseguest, I wanted to be gracious and give back to my friends. I asked myself, *How can I be of service to these dear people by doing something they would appreciate?* So, each morning, while they slept, I'd empty their ashtrays, which I felt good about doing. It was not a particularly fun task, but it was a gesture they wildly appreciated.

You might ask, "Aren't you enabling their nicotine habit?" No, and here's why: I was there for a social visit, not an intervention. They would've smoked like chimneys whether or not I cleaned their ashtrays, and they had no desire to stop drinking. This is different from enabling, which is when you worsen or cover for someone's dysfunctional behavior; I just wanted to make their lives a little easier.

In the end, we had a fantastic time, sharing meals, walking by the ocean, and just being together. Still, I must admit that it was a relief to say goodbye and reenter the glorious sober realms of fresh air and sweet smells in my own home.

In some situations, you can only give so much. I know that you may want to help others heal their various problems but also consider what's realistic. Remember, giving isn't always about you. It's also about what others can accept at that point in time.

It's exciting to update your giving habits. Spend some time journaling about your relationships. Which ones are healthy? Which are codependent? List a few constructive steps to rebalance codependent relationships such as checking up less on an anxious relative, setting a clear boundary, or letting others make and learn from their mistakes. Then, one by one, begin to reshape your codependent relationships and enjoy your well-balanced ones.

How to Empathize Without Taking on People's Stress

A dread that many of my patients share is, "What if people ask for more than I can give? I feel guilty if I say no."

To be of service you don't have to give 100 percent or more to everyone in need. At times, it's okay not to be so available. To stay centered sometimes you need to leave the mundane world for a while by taking a break from daily responsibilities to practice self-care. Give yourself that gift. When being of service, consider each situation individually. Always factor in your own energy level and physical and emotional limitations to assess how much you have to give. These considerations don't make you selfish. They make you smart. Of course, there are instances when service may involve enormous sacrifice such as when you're a caregiver, which I will discuss later on. Generally, though, healthy giving nurtures you too.

Described below are five strategies to support healthy giving.

1. Give a Little, Not a Lot

Appreciate the power of offering small gifts: a hug, a flower, a fresh salad, a birthday card, three minutes of your time instead of an afternoon. Some people limit their giving to an hour daily. Train yourself to be a high-quality giver in smaller increments when possible.

2. Set Compassionate, Guilt-Free Limits

If you feel you should say yes to every request, practice setting limits. You can respond, "I'm sorry, I'm unable to attend, but I appreciate the invitation," or "Thank you for asking, but I can't take on more commitments now," or "I'd love to help, but I only have an hour." If you feel guilty about setting limits, it's okay but set a limit anyway. Changing your behavior and taking action despite your fears and reservations can precede an attitude shift. You don't need to be guilt-free to set limits.

3. Go into Unavailable Mode

It's not healthy to be on call for others all the time. To preserve your energy, for minutes, hours, or longer, turn off your electronic devices, don't answer calls, and stop "doing favors" for others. This gives you a break to be demand-free. It may be surprising to realize that most people can survive without you for a while.

4. Recognize When You've Had Enough

There are some limits to giving you can't modify because your mental or physical health depends on maintaining them, and there is no way to compromise anymore. One friend told me, "I divorced my husband because I never wanted children and realized he'd always be one—a really high maintenance one." This was a positive decision for her. Sometimes protecting yourself requires a big change. Though achieving closure can be difficult, it's wise to lovingly acknowledge that it's time to move on.

5. Meditate and Pray

When there's nothing more you can do to help someone or they refuse help, remember to pray for their well-being and the best outcome to their problem. It's better to keep this prayer general rather than specific. In instances when you can't heal yourself or others—and you can't get rid of pain—turn the problem into a creative offering to the forces of love and healing. Allow them to work their magic. I also offer my adaptation of the Serenity Prayer:

> Grant me the serenity
> To accept the people or things I cannot change
> The courage to change what I can
> And the wisdom to know the difference.

If you're working too hard to help someone, take a pause. *Let the person be themselves without making it your mission to improve them.* As one patient vowed, "I'm going to stop trying to love the red flags out of others." There is a time to give and a time to replenish yourself. Healthy giving is graceful and patient and makes you smile—a healing gift to yourself and others.

The Devotion of Caregiving

Caregiving is an opportunity to help someone with a physical, emotional, or spiritual infirmity. It is a chance for your empathy to shine. Whether you are a part- or full-time caregiver, others are dependent on you so they may feel like they are in a more vulnerable state with many needs.

I know well how being a caregiver can be a crash course on empathy, self-care, and learning to delegate. I oversaw the care of both my parents, at different times, when they became ill and eventually passed away. This sacred responsibility stretched my heart and triggered a range of emotions I didn't even know I had. Clearly, I wasn't a child anymore. Of course, I knew that intellectually. But there's something so final about sitting at a parent's sickbed and becoming the decision-maker. With poignant lucidity and sadness, my mother told me a few months before her death, "The time for supporting you and listening to your problems is over. I must channel all my energy into fighting cancer now." She and I were in an entirely new territory where our parent-child roles were reversed.

As a caregiver, sometimes you see and feel things you never wanted to see or feel—but there they are. For months, I watched my mother suffer terrible pain and anguish as she became less the "self" I was used to. My empathy for her bore right through me, her pain inflaming my pain. Exhaustion, numbness, fear of abandonment, anger at the loss, admiration, love, and devotion all rushed through me. I wondered, *How much can one person feel?* Many of my insecurities that had lurked beneath my competent exterior arose from the depths. My healing lesson was to have compassion for myself.

Fast forward five years. As my father's caregiver, I watched him slip into dementia and lose his mobility from Parkinson's disease. I was blessed to be at his deathbed when he passed. It was a most intimate, painful, and touching experience. Above all, what I felt was love.

In the 1990s, when both parents became ill at different points, I hadn't learned the grounding and protection skills such as shielding and centering that I now have. These could have helped me replenish myself. As an only child without relatives nearby, it was a lot for me—or for any one person. But I also learned to call on professional helpers who were a godsend. These compassionate souls sat with each parent so I could rest or see patients or walk on the beach.

I am thankful that I could bring my mother and father more peace and stability in their final days. They didn't have to be alone or without the eyes of love. I was their advocate, their rock; a familiar, caring face in the storm. My father told others, "Judith is holding me under her wing."

If you're lucky to live long enough, you may be called on to be a caregiver for an aging loved one. I can't fully prepare you for the mammoth experiences and changes you can go through, but I can say that being my parents' caregiver was one of the most important roles I've ever had. It helped me open my heart, surrender fear, and be of service to the precious and imperfect people who had raised and cherished me.

Practical Tips for Caregivers

Empathy for yourself lets you be present for another. Healthy giving means sometimes stepping away from the person you are helping to meditate, sleep, attend to your own health, watch a funny movie, or talk to a friend. Also snuggle with your animal companions or stuffed animal friends to nourish your inner child who often gets lost in the caregiving process. In addition, whether you're assisting an immobile friend with a broken leg or helping a parent navigate an illness or end of life, here are five practical tips to follow.

1. Beware of Smothering Generosity

Sometimes you can help too much and smother people with generosity. Though you mean well, without knowing it you become intrusive, hovering, or nervously fussing over someone. You infantilize them by frequently asking, "Are you any better, honey? Are you in pain?" From the recipient's perspective, it can feel like you are treating them as a sick, helpless baby. *This is not a helpful message to convey if someone is dependent on you.* Of course, you don't want to minimize their suffering. But when you look at an ailing person, see their strengths and mirror everything that is most alive in them so they can see it too.

2. Appreciate the Pros and Cons of Being a Super-Giver

Being a super-giver offers you a sense of purpose in that you're contributing to someone's life. Also, there are real benefits for the recipient. Super-givers have high energy. They get things done and advocate for a patient. One recovering cancer survivor told me, "A super-giver helped me through the initial phases of treatment by staying on top of every detail."

Even so, super-givers can overcompensate for their fear of abandonment or rejection by doing too much. Their subconscious motive is that by making themselves indispensable, there's less chance that the person will leave them. In reality, this isn't always true.

If you are a super-giver, enjoy your assets but honor your own well-being too. You may be energized during a crisis but crash when it's over. At those times, it's therapeutic to stare at the wall and sleep as long as necessary. Stay balanced so that you can take care of yourself and help another without becoming resentful.

3. Know the Difference Between Worry and Concern

Worry is when you focus your anxiety on a specific target such as the health of the person you are caring for. Being someone who chronically worries may be an attempt to gain control or overcome a sense of helplessness about a situation.

You also may fear that if you don't worry, you aren't being caring enough or something bad will happen—a superstitious or culturally ingrained belief. For instance, I have a friend who was raised by a Jewish mother like mine who could've been a professional worrier. Once when my partner called her to say hi she breathlessly answered the phone, "What's wrong? Are you and Judith okay?" He replied, "Nothing is wrong. Why did you think that?" She said, "You never call me." Oy vey! Worry was a daily event in both our households growing up, and it permeated our lives.

Naturally, legitimate concerns arise when someone is ill, but *worry takes concern into the area of suffering.* To worry is to be human. However—and I know this may be hard to absorb— *worry doesn't help.* If you're climbing a mountain today and worrying about all the stressful things that could happen tomorrow, it will be a very difficult climb.

So, as a caregiver, if you must worry, take a deep breath then gently exhale it into the air. Stay in the Now rather than projecting your worries into the future. Stay focused on the moment so the task at hand seems more doable. Approaching the ailing person with a relaxed attitude and unworried eyes will help them worry less and heal faster.

4. Cultivate Tolerance and Patience

People who are suffering from acute or chronic pain or illness or are immobile can be irritable or just in a plain mean mood. During my UCLA psychiatric residency, I learned from hospital staff veterans that the meanest patients lived longer; the nice ones more easily slipped away. I'm not condoning meanness, but it is sometimes how seriously ill patients fiercely cling to their life force.

Still, if you're caring for someone who is cranky or mean, try to understand what's going on. Particularly if the person is dying, cut them some slack and stop trying to change them. They deserve to pass over in any way they choose, even if it is difficult for us to cope with or watch.

Tolerance means being able to "live and let live" without correcting someone's beliefs or behavior. With caregiving, it may mean tolerating someone's frustrating attitude or ongoing pain. Be patient with them. The guidelines for setting healthy boundaries throughout this book will also protect your energy.

Equally important, be patient with yourself. You are in a demanding situation and may encounter daily episodes of high drama. It's okay to feel tired and short-tempered. If caregiving gets to be too much, take a short break to find your center. Remind yourself, *I am an empathic person who is doing my best.*

5. Reach Out for Support and Resources

If you're helping someone who is chronically ill or terminal, it is lifesaving for you to seek help and to delegate. I understand the impulse to want to do everything yourself. After all, you are the person who knows and loves the patient the most—and you may feel uncomfortable bringing in a "stranger." Still, your healing involves learning to reach out for support.

There are many ways to do this. If you can afford a part- or full-time professional helper, utilize their services to free up space for you. Or find someone who can periodically clean the house. This will provide more peace of mind and a less chaotic environment.

Support groups for caregivers are available through local churches, synagogues, or other spiritual centers such as Unity churches. Additional resources include cancer or bereavement support groups. NAMI, the National Alliance on Mental Illness, offers a helpline that connects you to services if you're caring for those with mental illness.

If you're not a "joiner" or "group person," you might feel more comfortable with online support. You can participate in Zoom or phone meetings where you can simply listen. It might not feel like second nature to reach out in this way. Still, it is essential for your mental and physical health to find others who understand what you are going through.

When Caregiving Ends

The time may come when it's no longer necessary for you to be a caregiver. Sometimes this transition can be a grieving process that involves releasing the trauma you witnessed. This phase is done. You must move on. But how? You may have an identity crisis and wonder, *Who am I without this role?* Feel all the emotions that arise, seek support when you need it, and reclaim the part of yourself that has been dedicated to supporting another. This will keep you from staying stuck in caretaker or survival mode.

For a few intense months, I gave my all to helping a relative recover from back surgery. Happily, her healing process progressed to a point where she didn't require my assistance anymore. It was natural for me to experience fatigue and also a letdown when the caregiving experience ended. But to replenish myself, I also needed to reclaim the huge amount of energy that I had directed toward her. So in meditation, I consciously asked for that energy—which was about 20 percent of my total reserves—to return to me. I told myself the truth: *She is much better now and has adequate support. My job as caregiver is done.* This reconnected me with my full vitality and allowed me to find closure to this period.

Typically, caregiving has a beginning and an end. As you transition into the role, have empathy for yourself. As you transition out of the role, have empathy for yourself. Never forget that this is a momentous experience. Remember to look up at the stars and the heavens to know you are never alone. There will be an invisible hand guiding you if you can allow yourself to feel it.

EMPATHY IN ACTION

Meditation for Caregivers

In the quiet of your home or a safe place, breathe in deeply, then exhale completely. With compassion, let yourself locate any stress that has accumulated in your body. Are your shoulders or neck tense? Is your mind blurry? Do you feel tired or irritable? It's all to be expected. Have empathy for every ache or pain, for every flash of anxiety, worry, depression, or exhaustion you feel. Breathe love into each one. Be patient with yourself. You are being of service to another, a glorious act of empathy. Reconnect with your own energy and spirit. You are growing. You are giving. You are evolving your heart. Feel the poignancy and power of this opportunity.

8

Narcissists, Sociopaths, and Psychopaths

What Is an Empathy Deficient Disorder?

SOME PEOPLE ARE NOT wired neurologically or emotionally to have empathy. Behavioral scientists define this condition as an "empathy deficient disorder" where someone focuses on their own needs and neglects or doesn't care about the feelings of others. Those with empathy deficient disorder lack a moral compass.

I will train you to recognize these damaging and cleverly deceptive personalities, all of whom can be bullies. Then you won't be seduced by their charm or empty promises. To protect your own empathy, you must realize that *they are not your allies*.

Still, I've seen how many of my compassionate patients struggle to even compute that someone is incapable of empathy. Like them, you might think, *How can that be?* You may assume, *If only I did _____, I could help heal them, and they'd change*. I wish that were true, but I know from my years of clinical experience, it is not (though we are always learning more about empathy deficient disorders).

You may not realize that if a loved one or colleague has empathy deficient disorder, there could be no "there" to get through to.

Some of my patients have too much empathy for these individuals and remain in a state of denial. They tell me, "I hear you, Judith. But _____ is an exception. They've had such a sad childhood. I can sense their true potential." So, with the best intentions, my patients keep trying to win the love or heal the pain of these people and suffer greatly in the process until they reach rock bottom with the relationship and eventually let go. Certainly, it's tough to give up on someone or to see their deficiencies, but having misplaced empathy for those who can't reciprocate won't turn them into the heartfelt person you'd hoped for. Like my patients, you might never grasp how someone can truly lack empathy, but at least you can accept the reality of the situation.

So, as part of your learning curve, let's explore the nature of an empathy deficient disorder, how to identify these traits in others, and ways to protect yourself. Keep in mind that people with empathy deficient disorder, such as those with narcissism, want you to recognize how powerful they are whereas truly caring people want you to see how powerful you are.

The Empathy Spectrum

It's useful to think of empathy as a spectrum. In the middle are people with the admirable quality of "everyday empathy," the caring impulse to feel for others. On the next level up are highly sensitive souls who feel life intensely but tend to also be overwhelmed by sensory overload such as noise or light. Empaths are at the top of the spectrum. They have all the traits of highly sensitive people but may be sponges for others' emotions. At the lower end of the spectrum are those with empathy deficient disorder. These are the narcissists, sociopaths, psychopaths, and bullies we will discuss.

> There is no wrong path if you learn from it. Some paths are just more painful than others.

Who you have a relationship with is your choice. But like many people, particularly if you try to see the best in others, you might never have been educated about empathy deficient disorders. An ongoing theme of *The Genius of Empathy* is valuing your own needs and setting limits with destructive or otherwise hurtful or negligent people. Too many children and adults are trapped in unhealthy relationships and suffer tremendously. If you've made bad relationship choices in the past, you'll learn to be smarter now. This chapter is your guide to identifying and coping with people with an empathy deficient disorder.

Type 1. The Narcissist

In this section, I am referring to people with narcissistic personality disorder, or NPD, not those with a few narcissistic traits who may have some capacity for empathy and growth if they do the psychological healing work.

Like Narcissus, the tragic figure in Greek mythology who fell in love with his own reflection in a pond, narcissists are in love with themselves. Everything is all about them. In any encounter there is only one person present—and it isn't you! Though some people with narcissism are unlikeable and put you off with their giant egos, most can be intelligent, witty, exciting, and charming. They are skilled at reading a room. As expert seducers, they attract you by telling you exactly what you want to hear, including that your relationship with them has incredible promise.

Unconsciously or deliberately, they know how to channel heart energy. In fact, they often use love bombing, a seduction technique that for the short term makes you feel so special that you become compliant. Love bombing can include compliments, gifts, apologies for bad behavior, expressing intense feelings quickly, constant texting or calling, or saying all the words you ever dreamed of hearing. People with narcissism might appear empathic or even present themselves as your savior, conveying, *I have the answers to your problems*, but they are masters at creating a false front.

Their relationships are transactional: "I'll do this for you if you do this for me." A typical pattern of someone who has narcissism is to idealize you, then devalue you, then finally discard you. If you disagree with them or resist their plan, they become cold, withholding, and punishing, which feels like abandonment. Then you have to win back their approval. They exhaust you with all the hoops you must jump through to please them. Also, they may gaslight you by making you think your reaction is "crazy," so you doubt yourself. For instance, if your spouse had an affair, they might deny it, even if they got caught, or they might claim, "You're being paranoid and exaggerating the situation. We just had coffee together."

In addition, they commonly manipulate by using a psychological defense known as projection. If you say, "I feel hurt by your anger," they will use it against you, and say, "I'm not angry. You are." Then, if you question them or stick up for yourself, they'll make it known directly or indirectly, "It's my way or the highway." Understandably, these attitudes don't bode well for intimacy.

They often repeat the same toxic message over and over again, such as "You're so incompetent," until you actually believe it. Repetition is a well-known persuasive technique often used by advertisers. According to psychological studies, repeating simple words and phrases can convince people that they are true when they aren't.

Famous historical examples of leaders with narcissistic personality disorder include Julius Caesar, Napoleon, and Marie Antoinette, who notoriously ignored the needs of starving Parisian "commoners," which helped prompt the French Revolution.

People with narcissism often have most or all of the following traits. Even if someone has only one or a few, it's likely they have some narcissistic tendencies.

> ## Common Traits of Someone with Narcissism
>
> - Needs admiration, compliments, and validation
> - Is grandiose, manipulative, and entitled
> - Lacks empathy
> - Dominates and devalues others
> - Throws emotional crumbs to keep others hooked in
> - Gaslights and lies
> - Sets off love bombs
> - Punishes others with coldness, the silent treatment, and other forms of abandonment

Narcissism can fall into two main categories: the grandiose (overt) type and the vulnerable (covert or closet) type. The grandiose type is the obvious one we usually think of. They like to boast and be the center of attention, feel self-important, and surround themselves with "loyal" people who only agree with them. They may be obsessed with looks, success, and wealth. Often, they project the image of being wonderful to the world but privately they mistreat and exploit their loved ones. Some exude a charisma that makes you feel intoxicated and off-center.

In contrast, the vulnerable type is more hidden, subtler, and trickier to recognize since they prefer to stay out of the spotlight. They may be withdrawn because of their insecurities, low self-esteem, anxiety, or depression. Even though their vulnerabilities are real, they also can use them to manipulate others. Like a wolf in sheep's clothing, they may appear sweet, even shy, self-effacing, and caring.

But later they use generosity to control you, so that you feel you're indebted to them. Your gratitude and neediness feed them. They may also play the "victim" by appealing to your sympathy.[1]

There are various degrees of narcissistic personality disorder ranging from lacking empathy and being manipulative to the most abusive, aggressive, and sadistic versions of either the grandiose or vulnerable type. As spiritual leader Paramhansa Yogananda said about certain destructive personalities, "Some people try to be tall by cutting off the heads of others."[2]

**When you come home from a long day at work,
a narcissist probably won't ask you,
"How did your day go?"**

What Is Narcissistic Supply?

People with narcissism primarily want to wield power over others, not share affection, love, or differing points of view. They are fed by praise, empathy, attention, and your compliance and adoration. They have an insatiable need to be recognized for their greatness, which is known as "narcissistic supply."

They feel powerful when deceiving and manipulating you, a sense of dominance that feeds their supply. The more confused and emotionally triggered you are, the better. They love to see you lose your grounding, which communicates how in control they are. Narcissists also get their supply met through seduction, anger, punishment, and bullying. Their lack of empathy makes it easy for them to mistreat people without remorse.

Causes of Narcissism

What factors contribute to narcissism? Are people with narcissism born or made? In fact, both upbringing and genetics play a role.

Narcissism is linked to an early attachment trauma in which a child isn't healthily bonded, loved, or protected by their parents (whose style may be overprotective or neglectful). So they cope by developing survival skills such as manipulating and controlling people and their environment. Parental role modeling may also be a factor. Some children mimic the behavior of their narcissistic parents. In addition, research indicates that certain traits are genetically inherited, such as grandiosity and entitlement.[3] All the causes of this disorder aren't yet fully known, and research continues to be done in this area.

Someone with narcissism would never ask, "Am I a narcissist?" They believe nothing is their fault.

Can Narcissism Be Cured?

I've seen that it is difficult, if not impossible, to make progress with a narcissist in psychotherapy. They may learn to adapt so they appear less controlling and selfish, but add a little pressure or disappointment, and their manipulative behaviors usually reemerge.

The American Psychiatric Association's *Diagnostic and Statistical Manual of Mental Disorders* (DSM-5) categorizes those with narcissism along with sociopaths (psychopaths are not included in this manual) as personality disorders that are stubborn conditions to treat. Typically, these people can't or won't be accountable for their part in any conflict, so they blame others. Their attitude is, "Who, me? I didn't do anything wrong." *People with narcissism either believe their own lies or feel that it is their right to spread them.* If they are to have any hope of improving, they must work with a psychiatrist or other mental health professional who is trained in treating narcissism. I've seen too many inexperienced therapists get played by narcissists and end up believing their side of the story and demonizing their partners, associates, or family members.

Trauma therapies, including eye movement desensitization and reprocessing, or EMDR, may help people with narcissistic traits. Some psychoanalysts feel that entering analysis for many years can be useful for those with narcissism. In addition, twelve-step programs can also be helpful for some narcissists. Programs such as Alcoholics Anonymous (AA) and Al-Anon emphasize humility and service. People with narcissistic personality disorder can gradually learn, at least in part, to be giving and tolerant—and catch themselves when they are not. One thirty-year AA member, a former hustler, cocaine addict, and admitted narcissist, told me that prior to getting clean, he never even registered that others had needs too! Now he makes it a point to help at least one person every day.

How to Protect Yourself from a Narcissist

If you are involved with someone who has narcissism, especially a person from whom you can't escape, such as a supervisor, coworker, or relative, have empathy for yourself. If you get caught in their manipulations, simply regroup and begin again. Recentering yourself makes your choices clearer. You can also follow these eight steps to protect yourself:

1. Identify the frequent statements that people with narcissism make:

   - "How can I benefit?" or "What's in it for me?"

   - "All of my exes are crazy."

   - "You're overreacting. I didn't say that."

   - "You always take it the wrong way."

   - "You're being irrational."

- "What's the matter with you?"

- "Aren't I more important than your friends?"

- "It's not my fault. You made me do it."

2. Notice if someone exhibits these narcissistic behaviors:

   - Talks only about themselves without asking about you

   - Has a superior attitude and offers unsolicited advice

   - Blames or shames you

   - Lacks empathy for your pain and turns the conversation back to their own suffering

   - Shows little interest in you unless they want something

3. Create a minor disagreement.

   If you're uncertain whether someone has narcissism, provoke a small conflict. They are usually agreeable if they get what they want. But when you say no, narcissists aren't so nice anymore. If you tell them, "I can't get together tonight," they might retaliate with, "You don't value our relationship," or become unkind and blaming. Their reaction will help you accurately assess the person. (You may feel more comfortable doing this under the guidance of a therapist to offer you support.)

4. Release denial.

   You may make excuses for them or keep hoping that their behavior will change. Instead, see the situation realistically, even if it's painful, so you can practice self-care.

5. Reduce your expectations.

   You will always be emotionally alone with a narcissist. Accept that they can't give you unconditional love or empathy. Turn to others for nurturing and intimacy.

6. Don't make your self-worth dependent on them.

   Since people with narcissism want power over you, they'll often put you down to achieve it. Beware of trying to win the caring you never got from your parents. Know your own worth rather than looking to them for validation.

7. Feed their egos.

   With a boss, an in-law, or another person you can't leave, show how your idea will be to their benefit. Stick to facts, not emotions. For instance, "Your business will have a financial advantage if I take a vacation on these dates." As tedious as stroking their ego is, your request will more often get met with this technique.

8. Be aware of your emotional triggers.

   Don't fight with people who have narcissism—that only feeds their supply. If you're triggered, pause, breathe, and exit the encounter as soon as possible so you can center yourself before reacting.

Ending a Relationship with a Narcissist: Cutting Off Their Supply

If you're ready to say goodbye to someone with narcissism, realize that you will meet resistance. *When their supply is withdrawn, they get desperate and may stop at nothing to get what they want.* Rarely do they leave peacefully. They won't say (and mean), "I understand and support your decision. I'm sorry I hurt you." Instead, they will try to make you doubt your reasons for leaving.

Abandon all hope that someone with narcissism will change.

Sensitive, loving people waste lots of empathy trying to understand narcissists or give them the benefit of the doubt. They stay in the relationship for too long, hoping that the person will change. Empathizing with someone who isn't interested in changing is counterproductive. In these relationships, you need to save yourself first. Stop trying to fix the person or express your emotions. Instead, channel all that empathy toward your own healing so you can find mutually caring relationships.

Self-empathy means saying to yourself the following:

- *I didn't do anything wrong. I am not to blame for getting lured into this situation. I was never educated about narcissism.*

- *I have been through agony. I'm exhausted. I'm worn down. I've tried hard enough to make this relationship work. Now that I'm leaving, I must rejuvenate myself and let my healing process begin.*

To regain your power and shift the dynamic as you end the relationship, set clear limits and stick to them. If you still must have contact with the narcissist, regularly state your needs. Remain neutral. If you can't fulfill a request they make, say a centered, definite no. For example, "No, I can't be around you if you are unkind or dumping anger." Whatever your list of nos may be, begin to confidently express them.

The grey rock method can also help you cope with narcissistic manipulations. Your goal is to become nonreactive, like a grey rock. Avoid continued eye contact or physical interaction such as obligatory hugs or handshakes. Remain firm and unflappable.

Don't let yourself be triggered or create drama. These people feed on conflict and outbursts. If there is a problem to solve, be solution-oriented and keep interactions short. Limiting exposure and not taking the bait cuts off their narcissistic supply and reduces their destructive behavior.

Sometimes complete closure is possible; for instance, if you don't have children in common, or the person with narcissism isn't a coworker, colleague, or relative with whom you must interact. You may also choose to distance yourself from more peripheral contacts such as service providers. Just because you have gone to them for years doesn't mean you have to stay.

If there aren't ties that bind you to a partner with narcissism, and you are ready to leave, the cold turkey approach is best. This means no contact. Don't check their social media accounts to see what they're doing. Block them on these sites as well as on your phone. Then you won't need to contend with their mind games or temptations to stay. You are free.

When you go cold turkey, you'll have to endure the discomfort and cravings associated with leaving this relationship. It can feel like withdrawing from a heavy drug. Be ready for this. Keep breathing through the pain. It will get better.

To support yourself, don't hesitate to reach out to a therapist or coach who specializes in narcissism and trauma recovery. Also, you can participate in no-cost twelve-step support groups for forming healthier relationships such as Codependents Anonymous (CODA), which is available online and in person. Receiving encouragement and support will make your journey easier.

How Long Does It Take to Heal from a Narcissistic Relationship?

Recovering from this relationship includes recovering your self-empathy too. When you first leave, it is common to feel a huge rush of relief. Then a crash occurs when your fear, anger, desire for revenge, and self-doubt may creep in. These feelings are natural but remember that being happy can be the best revenge. Allow your emotions to surface in the safe container of your journal or with a compassionate listener. Don't act on them or express them to the narcissist. The more distance you get from them, the faster you will heal.

What is the timeline for healing? In the first days and months after separating, I've watched patients experience welcome relief for fleeting moments, then hours, then more. As time passes, the relief lasts longer. Their self-esteem rises if they stick with this approach and keep showing themselves empathy.

To help you successfully separate from a narcissist, also use the following cutting-the-cord visualization adapted from *The Empath's Survival Guide*. This exercise will help you release the relationship and remove any lingering connection you feel.

Cutting the Cord

In a calm state, visualize streams of light connecting both of you. Assert aloud or inwardly, "This relationship is over. It is time to cut our bonds now and forever." Then, picture yourself taking scissors and cutting each bond completely so all energetic ties are gone.

The next phase of healing is to focus on the kind of life you want to create. Once you leave, don't dwell on the past or on what the person is thinking or who they are with. Direct all your positive thoughts and actions to doing good for yourself and the world.

Manipulation Techniques to Watch For

If you're ready to say goodbye, realize that people with narcissism may amp up their considerable powers of seduction and persuasion to change your mind. However, when the onslaught begins, don't waiver. Stay strong and consistent. Watch for these mind games that they use to control you.

Hoovering

Looking utterly sincere, a partner might keep trying to lure you back with empty promises such as, "I can't live without you," "I'll go into therapy," or "I'll spend more time with you and the kids. I'll change." They relentlessly try to wear down your resistance.

Or they send a text that makes you feel special such as, "I miss seeing you. I'm thinking about you." You wonder, *Maybe they really do value our relationship* or *They've been so mistreated in the past, they didn't really mean to call me "stupid."* So you second-guess yourself and the next thing you know, you're in the clutches of this relationship again.

If you don't respond, they may increase the intensity of hoovering by showing up at your home unannounced, sending flowers or gifts, or calling you and either hanging up or leaving multiple messages. They may even hire a private detective to track your activities to find incriminating evidence to use against you.

False Flattery

People with narcissism believe that others are as receptive to flattery as they are. So they build you up to get you to do their wishes. They will use sweet talk to take advantage. If you are self-conscious about being shy and introverted, they might say, "I love quiet and thoughtful people. These are such rare traits." Or, if you feel unappreciated at work, they might say, "You are so respected in your field. I really admire you." Of course, being appreciated feels great, but this strategic flattery lays it on too thick. They only use it to manipulate and draw you back in.

Negging

Negging is a term that has recently arisen in popular culture and social media. It occurs when someone gives you a backhanded compliment or sends a mixed message such as, "You look so much more attractive now. Are you working out?" You think, *Huh? What did they mean by that?* Negging is used to undermine your confidence and make you question your resolve. If you are constantly trying to decode someone's comments or behavior, it could be a sign of negging.

Turning Loved Ones or Others Against You

People with narcissism play dirty. When you resist their manipulations, they might threaten to undermine your relationships or status in the community. Making your life miserable restores their sense of power over you. Since they have an empathy deficient disorder and lack a conscience, they aren't disturbed by hurting you. In fact, they feel justified in doing so.

Therefore, they won't hesitate to bad-mouth you to your children, colleagues, or whoever will listen. Or they will spread lies to get loved ones on their side such as calling you an "unfit parent," "selfish," or "irresponsible." As part of their defamation campaign, they will fight for custody of the kids and limit your visitation rights. Then, on the days you have the kids, they will "forget" to show up. These maneuvers boost their sense of importance and control, which keeps feeding their supply.

**You can't beat a narcissist at their game.
You simply must not play it with them.**

Although it may feel that my approach goes against your instinct to verbally fight back and protect yourself, realize that you *are* doing both but in more discerning and emotionally intelligent ways that weaken a narcissist's hold on you. You still assert your needs but remain centered rather than simply reacting to their antics.

Buddhism likens this sort of rigorous emotional practice to "learning to ride the wild ox backward." The ox is a symbol of stability, but in life, one must learn to calmly ride it (sometimes backward) in tumultuous circumstances as well as, more enjoyably, in times of grace.

While breaking free from the relationship, savor your baby steps of progress. If you can move back from the chaos and heartache of dealing with a narcissist, the experience becomes a worthy lesson in how to empathize with yourself, ward off the darkness in human nature, and know your own worth and inner power.

Type 2. The Sociopath and the Psychopath

People with narcissism and those with antisocial personality disorders (sociopaths) share many qualities such as having an inflated self-image, enormous powers of persuasion and manipulation, and a lack of empathy. This overlap is why such people are frequently diagnosed as both. However, not all people with narcissism qualify as sociopaths. Overall, sociopaths are known for their reckless, impulsive behavior. They get in trouble with the law and may land in prison. In contrast, narcissists are smoother operators who are motivated by a strong need to look good, appear successful, and be admired. Others' opinions matter more to a narcissist than to a sociopath.

Famous people with sociopathic personality disorder include Bernie Madoff, the money manager who swindled thousands of retirees and others out of their savings; Ted Bundy, a serial killer who lured victims in with charm; Aileen Wuornos, one of the most famous female murderers; and Charles Manson, the charismatic cult leader and killer. These infamous sociopaths and others with this disorder have the following similar characteristics.

Common Traits of a Sociopath

- Disregard social rules and are con artists
- Financially exploit you while getting excited from the game
- Experience no remorse for conning you
- Behave destructively and dangerously and exhibit thrill-seeking behavior
- Display anger and rage
- Recognize what they are doing but rationalize their behavior
- Can't maintain regular work or a family life

To determine if someone is a sociopath, pay attention to their behavior, not their words. Ask yourself, *Are they risk-takers? Would I ever do that? Is it safe?* With their charm, they might try to convince you that shoplifting is exciting or attempt to con you into a "sure thing" financial investment. Notice if they are willing to harm others to get what they want. Also check in with your intuition. Are you comfortable with their ideas? Do you get a "beware" signal in the pit of your stomach? If so, you might be dealing with a sociopath.

Another related charismatic empathy-deficient personality is the psychopath. They are an extreme, more lethal, cunning version of both a sociopath and narcissist, though they have no official diagnosis in the DSM-5. They may pretend to care but don't. Also, they sometimes maintain the façade of an ordinary family life as a front for criminal activity. They are masters of control and make cold-hearted killers. They murder more easily because they don't feel internal consequences. People who are psychopaths also have an uncanny ability to get you to abandon morality and common sense, so you submit to their domination.

What causes someone to become a sociopath or psychopath? Research suggests that brain defects and injuries as well as early trauma may contribute.[4] Others theorize that their autonomic nervous system, which triggers the fight-or-flight response, doesn't become as activated in threatening situations. Therefore, there are fewer "stops" on their behavior. Some research proposes that psychopaths aren't as responsive to the input of the relaxing vagus nerve, which helps create safety in relationships. Their muted emotional response to danger keeps them calm in situations where others would be afraid.[5] In fact, studies suggest that even if psychopaths seem agitated, they may become calmer internally when they are hurting others.[6]

Some say that sociopaths are made, and psychopaths are born.[7] People who are psychopaths have a lifelong pattern of behavior, but a sociopath's actions may be learned from situations such as being involved with the "wrong kids" in school or being raised in a culture that glorifies a criminal lifestyle, though these ideas are not agreed upon in all professional circles. I'm excited to see what new research can bring.

Though narcissists are more common than sociopaths and psychopaths, some similar guidelines for coping may apply. Ideally you can avoid such a relationship. There is not much of a "win" in it for you to get involved, no matter how seductive or convincing they may be. If they are a family member with whom you have continued contact, practice clear limit setting and don't get pulled into their financial or other criminal schemes. If they are your boss, it would be reasonable to look for another job and always refuse to participate in any shady business actions. Psychopaths, of course, may pose a physical danger to others and have a charismatic appeal that you must resist. Be wary of highly charismatic people until they prove they are reliable and that their actions match their words.

Dealing with Bullies

Serial bullies often show narcissistic, sociopathic, or psychopathic tendencies and also may have an empathy deficient disorder.[8] They can be grandiose and arrogant while belittling others' accomplishments or personal qualities.

People who bully are notorious for targeting people who they perceive as "different," weak, or flawed or who can't stick up for themselves. What do they want? Mainly, to have power over people (since deep down they feel powerless), which they get by denigrating and dehumanizing others.

What motivates bullying? A few factors include fear of people's differences, unresolved trauma, low self-esteem, a fragile ego, insecurity, and poor parental role modeling. Many bullies get pleasure from being cruel or seeking revenge. Unconsciously, someone who bullies can feel, *If I make you wrong, inferior, or "weird," my hatred, anger, and poor treatment of you is justified. Denying your worth and getting my friends to scapegoat you* (mob mentality) *gives me control over you.* Understanding this dynamic never justifies bullying behavior. It simply explains what motivates it and deadens their empathy. In psychiatric circles this defense mechanism to manage fear and trauma is known as depersonalization, where someone makes another unrelatable or inhuman. To protect your empathy and peace of mind, practice the following strategies with bullies.

Tips to Cope with People Who Bully

- Tell someone you can trust about the bullying behavior rather than keeping it secret because you're ashamed. Inform your parents, spouse, good friend, school counselor, or human resources at work who can offer support.

- Stop expecting the bully to have empathy for you—most don't.

- Give up trying to figure the bully out. Accept they are wounded and can do real harm.

- Do not react emotionally to the bully's tactics. They feel powerful by dominating others who are weaker. Stay calm. Leave the situation as soon as possible.

- If your relative is an emotional bully, sit next to someone else at a family dinner and have minimal contact if they won't stop.

- If the bully is your boss, you may need to discretely look for a new job.

- In instances of physical abuse and bullying, contact law enforcement and secure legal assistance to get a restraining order. Your resolve and refusal to cower helps to undermine a bully's game.

Healing Codependency

Sometimes you badly want to leave an unhealthy relationship, but you feel torn. A part of you longs to start fresh and move on, and another part keeps being drawn back to the person who hurts you. Don't be down on yourself. You can change and heal. To discover what prevents you from leaving and finding healthier connections, recognize these common blocks.

Wound Mate Relationships

In a wound mate relationship, you are locked into a defeating pattern where you bond with each other through your mutual wounds, trauma, and pain. This can feel intense and intimate, whether it's a romance or any potentially close relationship. But actually, you may be confusing intensity with intimacy and control with caring. You marvel at finding someone who is just like you and mistake them for a soul mate or soul friend. That's why people who misuse substances are often attracted to each other and to other "wounded birds." Or, yet again, you get involved with a narcissist who can manipulate your self-doubts and vulnerability, which draws you in.

My patient Lois described her painful choices in romantic partners. She said, "I feel I have more in common with people who've had a difficult childhood since I had one too. We 'get' each other." With such seeming rapport Lois was baffled about why the relationships failed. She didn't understand that the same emotional wounds could prevent a partner from showing healthy intimacy. Nor did she grasp that the sizzling chemistry that can come from having a common history can't always be equated with love. It often turns volatile and abusive with wound mates. So, in therapy, Lois started to accept that she was choosing wound mate relationships, which were unhealthy and painful. As she explored her own emotional patterns, such as needing to overgive to win someone's love, she became attracted to potential partners who were more capable of intimacy.

If you identify with being a wound mate, you can begin to heal this pattern in psychotherapy, as Lois did. As a result of her emotional growth, she was able to become a caring partner who is more capable of intimacy. Participating in a twelve-step recovery group for codependency, such as CODA, can help you choose healthier people too. However, if you haven't done this healing work, you could easily be drawn into these destructive relationships again, so be cautious.

Having empathy for someone's difficult past doesn't mean you accept their current abusive behaviors.

The first step to healing this pattern is to be aware of it. Gently explore any beliefs that keep you repeating harmful relationships. Record them in a journal. Common ones are, *I only connect intimacy with pain* and *A loving family yells at you because they care.* Tenderly replace these beliefs with more healing ones such as, *Love means mutual respect* or *Healthy intimacy feels comfortable and nurturing.* Have empathy for the beliefs that drew you to wound mates in the past so you can stay open to more emotionally available partners now.

Trauma Bonds and Neurochemicals

Trauma bonds are the ties that keep you hooked into wound mate relationships. For instance, people who have narcissism often use the technique of intermittent reinforcement to cement trauma bonds: they throw you crumbs of love and attention, then withdraw them. This ignites a craving response in your brain akin to addiction.

You may be attracted to what is familiar, not necessarily what is good for you. So, if one or both of your parents had narcissism, you may choose similar partners. You know what it's like to be thrown scraps of love and how the push-pull of receiving intermittent reinforcement feels. You stay in these relationships too long because you fear being alone, or you believe you can't make it without them. You also crave their approval. So as a trauma response, you may normalize hurtful behavior and continue trying to win their love.

The allure of slot machines is based on a similar intermittent reinforcement. In terms of the brain's neurochemical response, always winning wouldn't be nearly as addictive or exciting as not knowing if or when you might win. In relationships, this fluctuating cycle of kindness and neglect or abuse will alternate between producing oxytocin, which spikes with intimate bonding, and cortisol, which leads to burnout. The unstable chemical cocktail keeps you chronically anxious and wanting more.

People-Pleasing, Fawning, and Codependency

People-pleasing and fawning are forms of codependency where you ignore your own needs to avoid conflict and criticism and hyperfocus on others' needs. You become "too nice" and overly apologize for what is not your responsibility. You also find it hard to set boundaries. This is often a trauma response to coping with the controlling behavior of someone with narcissism. Being aware of this tendency will help you to be more loving with yourself as you set your intention to grow and change.

If you identify with the above patterns, have empathy for what you've been though and get ready to heal.

Realize that every person we meet along the way, loving or not, can help you grow. Do not beat yourself up for getting involved with someone who has empathy deficient disorder. Learn what you can from the situation, including setting healthy boundaries and saying no to abuse, so you don't repeat this lesson. It is emotionally liberating to heal an attraction to a person who is abusive so you can have more love and trust in your life. Treasure yourself. Know that you deserve respectful and caring relationships.

Having Empathy for Empathy Deficient People

Those with empathy deficient disorders and/or who bully can be treacherous since they may misconstrue your caring as a weakness that targets you for poor treatment. I've emphasized the importance of having empathy for yourself if you've endured such a relationship. What about empathy for their struggles and emotional traumas? Is that ever appropriate or healthy?

In these cases, empathy is never something you should do to be "socially correct." Like some of my patients, you may be adamant about never wanting to show empathy for these "monsters." Of course, that is your right. You're justified in feeling angry, hurt, and traumatized.

Even so, you may be at a place in your own healing where it feels intuitively right to try. You don't forgive or forget someone's behavior but rather find some empathy for these human beings who have deep emotional wounds. One patient shared that this attitude helps them remember that everyone has a backstory but not to be victimized by it. Then they can empathize with the ugliness of their behavior while also protecting themself. The point is not to excuse, but to understand the depth of their psychopathology.

Empathy sometimes means making radical choices, not ones that others usually make. Though empathizing with people who cause you suffering may not seem to make sense, it has unsuspected benefits as you heal from the relationship.

How does this work? The power balance shifts. Now you become the decider, the one who sets a higher tone. You're doing this mostly for yourself, not them. Choosing to shift the relationship's dynamic can begin to free you emotionally. You start to feel more distant from the trauma and less bound to the person who hurt you. You're not as stuck in your pain. You breathe more fully. And so, with great relief, it becomes easier to move on.

If you're a magnet for people with empathy deficient disorders—and many caring people are—it's time to reclaim your power. Beware of those who want to take it from you. Never act in a way that doesn't feel intuitively right. Don't obey anyone who wants you to break a law or break a heart or betray or harm someone or yourself. Those with empathy deficient disorders will take you down if you let them. So, don't let them.

Instead, gravitate toward people who are splashes of light in the human landscape. This means learning to connect to new love interests or friends who may not have the intensity or other trauma-bond "highs" that you could be used to. Instead, give new people a chance before writing them off as "nice but boring." Many trauma survivors mistake healthy for boring because they're not used to connecting to a caring, stable person.

You can shift this pattern by looking for people who are thoughtful, humble, and considerate. They follow through on promises and have good hearts. This doesn't mean that they don't have an edge or aren't passionate in their lives. Nor does it mean that they are perfect. But they are emotionally available to forge a healthy bond with you. Spend time with them so you can get used to feeling safe. Realize that the genius of empathy is about creating and flourishing in a safe environment with dependable people who respect your needs.

EMPATHY IN ACTION

Changing Patterns, Choosing Love

Take time to have empathy for yourself and the hurt that unhealthy relationships have caused you. Assure yourself that you are committed to healing and to practicing self-love. Feel your inner freedom growing. Have empathy for the part of you that didn't know better than to get involved with people with empathy deficient disorders. But now and in the future, feel gratitude for the new you who is prepared to never again give your power away to anyone.

PART 3

Healing
the
World

9

Empathic Leadership

The Strength of Leading
with Your Mind and Heart

THERE'S A HUNGER FOR empathic leadership in many organizations including corporations, governments, medical centers, and small businesses across the globe. Empathy is a game changer because we need kinder, people-sensitive work environments as well as a world with more warmth. My friend Rex Wilder, poet and master creator of slogans, says, "Humankind. Be both." That is our imperative, individually and as leaders, as well as the consistent call to action in this book.

Imagine a boss who takes time to listen to your needs and stands up for them. Imagine a team leader who can inspire you to be your most creative, productive, happy self. Or picture a manager who helps your team cooperate with each other and knows how to turn down the temperature in high-stress conflicts. All this is possible with the model of leadership I'm presenting.

Stress, burnout, and mental health concerns permeate workplaces today. In the post-pandemic era, many people are struggling to define what kind of job and setting—virtual, in person, or hybrid—makes the most sense for them. My patients Mary and Rick, who have two young children, prefer the freedom of virtual work since they can excel in their professions while being more present for their kids. Though global workplace policies remain in flux, both Mary and Rick's bosses continue to be accommodating and are showing greater empathy for other team members' needs.

At this crucial turning point, we need empathic leaders with innovative management styles to motivate teams and provide regular moments of connection and caring, as well as global leaders who can help create a more loving, unified, and cooperative world. Oprah Winfrey says, "Leadership is all about empathy. It's all about the ability to connect with people for the purpose of inspiring and empowering their lives."[1]

What Is an Empathic Leader?

Daniel Lubetzky, founder and CEO of KIND nutritional products, has said, "If you're asking how to create an empathetic workplace, you're ahead of everyone else."[2]

But how do you accomplish this? An empathetic leadership style values integrity and relating to others to understand their point of view. Empathic leaders take a genuine interest in team members. They want to know what makes them tick, what inspires them, and how they feel. They nurture their team's talents and strengths while using appreciation and positive reinforcement to encourage excellence.

For example, when an empathic leader sees a team member faltering, they don't crank up the pressure to perform or use criticism to motivate. Nor do they lead with impatience, which only makes people freeze or panic. Instead, they begin with appreciation for the person's contributions to the team. Then, in a caring tone, they address any difficulties they are encountering and explore strategies together to reach their goal. Approaching a team member with empathy rather than impatience does not make leaders pushovers, weak, or unable to set boundaries. Rather, they incorporate strength and empathy to lead.

Once when I was working on a project that required a series of meetings, I had to reschedule one date because a family member was having surgery the next day. I apologized to the project manager (who organized the schedule) for the change and any inconvenience it might have caused the team. Despite my efforts, he responded with no emotion in his voice, "Rescheduling would put the team back too far. It is best if you just go ahead with the meeting." I was stunned at what felt like a chilling response. True, I gave late notice because I had wrongly calculated my emotional bandwidth to both support my relative and be at the meeting. Still, canceling is not a pattern for me, but I was given no wiggle room. In the end, I did attend but honestly, it didn't feel great having my needs dismissed. Still, I didn't raise this with the manager since I wanted to focus on my relative and avoid a confrontation.

My message is that having more empathy for colleagues and team members can only help leaders. For instance, the project manager might have graciously led with, "Judith, I didn't realize that a family member was having surgery. We'll all be holding good thoughts for them. I will do everything possible to reschedule the meeting."

In the workplace, a little kindness goes a long way and creates goodwill. Sometimes we need to cut a coworker some slack even if it inconveniences us. When we do, they will remember the kindness, and it will bring the team closer together.

However, many employees may be understandably afraid to directly express their needs, especially with a nonempathic boss. So, they hold in their anger, shame, or frustration, which creates tension in their bodies and in the workplace via emotional contagion. Still, it's important to be discerning. If you are dealing with someone who is ordinarily caring, expressing yourself in a respectful, nonblaming way can be productive. Alternatively, if you have a boss with an empathy deficient disorder who may not value your needs, your effort may have no impact at all or it may antagonize them. In this situation, "managing up" may mean having realistic expectations of your boss so you don't keep expecting more than they can give.

Sometimes, though, even if you don't supervise others, you can take a leadership role by being a positive model for team members. For example, you step up to clarify your needs to a manager who you think would consider your point of view. If you receive a helpful response, it could inspire coworkers to speak up with discernment too.

I'm delighted that such a wide range of global, military, and workplace leaders have stressed the importance of empathy. These include former US Presidents Barack Obama and Abraham Lincoln, as well as Supreme Court justice Ruth Bader Ginsberg. Theodore Roosevelt said, "No one cares how much you know until they know how much you care."[3] Business leaders such as Sir Richard Branson also endorse empathy as does Mark Divine, a former Navy SEAL who writes about the power of leading from your heart.

Five Traits of Empathic Leaders

Empathic leaders . . .

1. **Lead by example**. They are role models for empathy and being collaborative. They let team members know, "I care about your concerns and values. Let's work this through together."

2. **Have emotional intelligence**. They think outside the box and encourage others' creative ideas. During a conflict they stay centered and combine logic and empathy to resolve the issue. They feel for others' dilemmas, but they can identify and control their emotions.

3. **Listen to their intuition.** They trust their gut in decision-making and support their team in doing so too.

4. **Show appreciation.** They let others know that they value their time, work, and contributions.

5. **Are flexible.** They quickly read others' needs and emotions and can adapt to a new or changing situation without becoming rigid or critical. These are vital qualities for crisis management.

Common Challenges Faced by Empathic Leaders

Leaders who are highly sensitive people may encounter challenges while managing their teams. Some find it hard to provide "constructive feedback" about the difficulties a team member is having with their work, since they want everyone to be happy and loathe hurting others' feelings. Still, they must learn this valuable communication skill.

For instance, as a supervisor, you observe that a team member is stuck in perfectionism, which limits their project's progress. You see them struggling and holding themselves to impossible standards. If you say nothing about this, it won't help them. Instead, you can take them aside and say in a supportive, noncritical tone, "You are an important member of our team. We love your ideas. But it looks like you're tripping yourself up by trying to be too perfect. Does that feel right?" Most likely it will, and you can discuss ways they can take the pressure off themselves. A gentle reminder from a thoughtful colleague can put them back on track to enjoying their work. Becoming comfortable with raising sensitive subjects is part of the learning curve for empathic leaders.

Such leaders must be prepared to contend with other people's outdated or biased beliefs about their style of leading. I'm moved by the candor of Jacinda Ardern, former prime minister of New Zealand, who said, "One of the criticisms I've faced . . . is that I'm not aggressive enough or assertive enough or maybe somehow because I'm empathetic, it means I'm weak. I totally rebel against that. I refuse to believe that you cannot be both compassionate and strong."[4]

Equating empathy with weakness is wrong. Empathy is a strength that comes from the heart, as opposed to force, which must always be a last resort. Rather than insisting an employee do something your way, you can model a smarter, kinder approach to problem-solving. You might say, "I understand this is a tedious project. Let me know how I can support you."

Why Is Empathic Leadership So Important?

I am excited to see that *Forbes* recently reported on a large research study that ranked empathy as the *most important* leadership skill in the workplace.[5] It has been shown to drive positive business results and has numerous therapeutic effects on stressed employees. When leaders expressed empathy for their team, it increased a team's innovation and engagement, improved customer service, and helped them balance their home and work life.

Sir Richard Branson said, "Understanding empathy, as well as the experiences of people from different areas of life, is a key skill for business leaders."[6]

With similar conviction, Satya Nadella, CEO of Microsoft, said, "Empathy makes you a better innovator. . . . It's a quality my wife helped me begin to learn when our son was born with severe disabilities. . . . It's a quality that shapes our quest to meet unmet needs of customers. And . . . it helps us as a society move forward in creating new opportunities for all."[7]

To further document empathy's advantages at work, the Global Empathy Index, which is published in the *Harvard Business Review*, examined data from employees' responses to questions ranging from a CEO's approval ranking to their own happiness level in their job. Researchers found that empathic companies are the most profitable and are associated with increased employees' earnings and gratification as well as customer satisfaction.[8]

You may be surprised to learn that the appeal of empathic leadership also extends beyond conventional office environments. In *The Way of the SEAL*, former Navy SEAL commander Mark Divine writes about how he trains athletes, SWAT teams, first responders, and aspiring SEALS to combine mental toughness with intuition and heart.[9] Empathic leadership is not only for supersensitive types. It is also for people with a range of temperaments in any field.

You can become an empathic leader, whether you're a new manager or a C-suite executive, or you're simply leading by example in any job even if you don't manage anyone. Since the need for empathy and human connection has increased in our chaotic world, the power of everyday empathic leadership has grown.

I offer empathy trainings to tech and other companies and medical settings. I teach teams and managers to bring empathy into the workplace and learn ways to compassionately address team members with difficult traits. Applying these skills can improve the atmosphere and health of any company.

In one training for hospital staff, Nora, who was a surgical nurse, and her supervisor, Linda, shared with the group that they were having problems communicating. I asked each of them to describe the difficulty. Every story has two sides. Nora said, "Linda asked for my help on a project but then became impatient when I took too long to answer her questions." She said Linda would snap, "Get to the point," which made Nora feel cut off.

Linda experienced Nora as "long-winded" but hadn't tried to resolve the issue since she avoided conflicts. Plus, Nora's lengthy explanations stoked Linda's anxiety about failing to meet the project's looming deadlines.

Nora admitted to having a slower, more methodical speech style but lamented, "Can't Linda just give me twenty seconds more to express myself? I want to help, but I feel my input isn't valued."

I worked with them both to develop empathy for each other's perspective. Linda admitted that she had felt so rushed and overloaded that she hadn't even considered how curt and unappreciative her tone sounded. In an effort to simply "get the job done" she didn't consider how her delivery affected Nora. To Linda's credit, after just a few minutes of defending her position, she became open to receiving this feedback and was willing to modify her behavior. Meanwhile, Nora could also see that her own longer explanations were making Linda impatient so she agreed to shorten them. So by honestly examining an unproductive pattern, both sides gave a little and also empathized with each other's needs—a start to more successful communication.

For over twenty-five years—ever since I graduated from my UCLA residency training—I've had the joy and satisfaction of supervising other psychiatric residents in that program. I feel privileged to be able to model empathy for them and show how they can incorporate it into their patients' treatment while also combining their linear, conventional psychiatric knowledge. We address a wide scope of topics from how to show empathy for difficult patients to having empathy for themselves during their rigorous, four-year, often sleep-deprived psychiatric training. I am honored that *The New England Journal of Medicine* wrote about my approach to modeling empathy for medical practitioners: "Her simple but powerful message is, 'Listen to your patients.'"[10]

In our high tech age, physicians often focus more on typing a patient's symptoms into a computer than offering their total attention.

When my skilled internist started doing this with me, he seemed only half-present during our visits. I mentioned how disconcerting this was. He responded thoughtfully, "I'm sorry. But there are new strict record-keeping requirements that I must adhere to. I can't input my notes later because my schedule is too busy." So unfortunately, the profound gift of fully listening was sacrificed in his medical practice, which prompted me to switch to another doctor who could be more present.

Eye contact, listening, and empathizing go together. Patients often feel vulnerable and scared when discussing their medical issues. They depend on their doctors and need them to be attentive and consoling.

Empathic leaders in medicine, the corporate arena, government, or other fields are ideally positioned to teach and model empathy for students and their teams. In fact, I propose that health care, technology, and other organizations have a chief empathy officer (or an entire empathy department), who could work with human resources to support employees. A chief empathy officer would help resolve conflicts in teams or among executives and other levels of management. So at work, you would have a safe place to find smart and caring solutions to a range of personal and organizational issues.

Mission-Focused Versus People-Focused Leaders

The old style of mission-focused leaders puts an organization's goals above people's needs. Employees must make work the top priority. The rest of their lives are often on hold until a project is completed. On the other hand, a people-focused approach makes the employees' needs a priority.

Let's compare the mission-focused model to the empathic style. The old model was built on the conventional sports paradigm where team members report to an all-powerful coach whom you don't question. You follow their directions implicitly.

Similarly in the workplace, this hierarchical, patriarchal system has leaders who run businesses with an authoritarian hand and not much empathy. They eliminate or demote employees who question them. The leader's message is, *I am the boss. You are the employee. Do what I say just because I tell you to.*

All this sets up a toxic, anxious atmosphere where narcissists, sociopaths, and other bullies flourish. As a result, in these work environments you'll find many unhappy employees whose job is drudgery. Work becomes only about earning a paycheck rather than experiencing any satisfaction or joy.

We love to hate the power-hungry characters with no empathy who portray old-style leaders in film and television. Take Gordon Gekko, the corporate raider in the iconic 1980s film *Wall Street* whose motto was "greed is good." Or Bobby Axelrod, the ruthless, charismatic hedge fund manager in the Showtime series *Billions,* which chronicles New York's brutal world of high finance.

May this cold, ego-driven model of doing business be replaced by a more empathic "style with a conscience" that brings out the best in executives, managers, and their teams. Thank goodness, lecturing to one's team, ordering them around, or ignoring their needs are approaches that are increasingly fading into the past, at least in some fields. These attitudes just alienate people, motivate them with fear, or fuel resentments. Instead, in a people-focused model, you meet employees where they are at and listen to them, so they feel safe enough to trust you.

What an uplifting way to bring more empathy into the work-place! So you are not just an employee whose role it is to earn money for the company. Rather, you are valued as a whole person. The guiding principle of a people-first philosophy is to treat others as you want to be treated.

Consider your response when a team member is frequently late to meetings. Instead of opening with the intimidating comment, "Don't you take your job seriously? You'll be fired if you can't show up on time," a people-first leader might say with genuine concern, "Hey Bill, is anything particularly stressful going on in your life? I noticed that you've been late a lot recently." Then they would help the employee solve the problem by saying, "I'm happy to address this issue with you."

In the best of worlds, people-focused values might not even need to be stated since they would be common assumptions. But now, as work cultures evolve, we must specifically prioritize the needs of each human being. Making this a policy creates an attitude of respect and comradery among the sacred group you call "my team." There is a magic to the forces that bring people together in work or in any circumstance. Try to see that magic in your team and in your collaborations.

Differences Between Old and New Paradigm Leaders

Old Style: Mission-Focused Leaders

- Value an organization's mission and bottom line above people's needs.
- Make decisions without considering the talented perspective of team members.
- Use blame and shame to motivate employees.
- Aim to "win" at any cost and reward ruthless ways of doing business.
- Fail to model or teach empathy as a relationship-building skill.

New Style: People-Focused, Empathic Leaders

- Put the needs of people first.

- Create a happy, even playful environment.

- Value collaboration, serving others, and an employee's experience.

- Help team members find the greatness within themselves.

- Replace dominance with empathy and heartfulness.

Practical Strategies to Address Stressful Work Situations

In the past twenty years, team building to increase bonding and appreciation, both in person and remotely, has become a common business practice. Now, many work cultures revolve around members being part of a team rather than relying on the older model of an individual employee who works independently and reports to one boss. So in the spirit of team building, below are five stressful situations you might face as an empathic leader and how to handle them in sensitive, efficient ways.

Situation 1. Handling Unexpected Work Assignments

When people are asked to do more than what was expected, and their workload is already demanding, the thought of doing more can trigger panic that spreads via emotional contagion to your team. An empathic leader remains calm. They compassionately acknowledge (but do not make excuses for) the reality of this stress and turn down the temperature on overwhelm and tension in an individual or a team.

What to Say

"It's clear to all of us that we are being asked to do more than we had planned. I know this feels overwhelming, but we will support each other as we get through it. I appreciate all of you. As a team, let's be especially kind to ourselves and each other during this demanding time."

What Not to Say

"Stop whining. You're required to do your work—so do it. Cancel plans with your family if necessary. Put in more hours until you finish."

Situation 2. Managing a Team Member's Unintentional Mistake

When someone makes a mistake, you want to lift them up instead of putting them down or increasing the pressure to perform. To gain empathy for the person, reflect on times when you have made errors, and how you would have wanted to be treated. Remember, no one is perfect. Of course, it feels frustrating when the error affects you and your work quality. Don't emotionally bypass that understandable feeling though it is unconstructive to come from that position when talking to the colleague. It will just make them feel worse. If you're clear about wanting to help them identify what happened, you can solve the issue with kindness.

What to Say

"I appreciate how hard you've worked on this project. I know you didn't mean to make this mistake. Let's figure out ways to prevent it from happening again."

What Not to Say

"How could you make this mistake? Your work is below company standards. You've put the whole team back since they depend on the information you provide."

Situation 3. Dealing with Failure and Underproducing

Sometimes a team member can go into a slump. Their creativity, sense of fun, and energy seem to fade. That's when an empathic leader can talk to them to find out what's happening. It's okay to say, "I noticed that you seem tired and less enthusiastic than usual. If you are open to discussing this, I'd like to hear what's going on. Then I can help."

In this way, the leader creates a safe, nonjudgmental opening for the team member to share. Perhaps they are worried because their spouse got fired and can't find another job. Or they are simply bored in their job and need a new project to feel more creative. By providing a safe place for them to share, you can find out how to support them and improve their work experience. If they choose not to share, simply wait and watch to see how their situation unfolds.

What to Say

"I care about you and want you to be happy at work. Lately, I've noticed a shift in your interest and energy. Your mind seems to be somewhere else. So I'm checking in to see how things are going. I would like to be supportive."

What Not to Say

"To be honest, I'm really concerned about your attitude and performance. You're not as productive as usual, and you look unhappy. You need to pull yourself together at work and leave personal problems behind."

Situation 4. Addressing a Team Member's Upsetting Behavior

Every team has members who can be argumentative, stubborn, critical, or defensive at times (as we all can be). Often, though, coworkers or managers may be wary of mentioning the problem to the person for fear of evoking their wrath or hurt feelings, or that they'll threaten to quit. Or, like many sensitive people, they can't tolerate making someone even slightly uncomfortable. So the troubling behavior becomes the elephant in the room that the team futilely tries to ignore. An empathic leader is prepared to compassionately discuss the specific behavior with the person. They are strong enough to tolerate discomfort, especially when they are showing tough love.

What to Say

"I've noticed that you are gossiping about Mike losing his promotion. I'm sure you do not purposely want to harm him, but gossip is hurtful and unacceptable. It can poison our workplace. I respect you and I want us to address and resolve this issue together."

What Not to Say

"How can you be so thoughtless and mean? You know Mike feels awful about losing the promotion. What's wrong with you? You should be ashamed of yourself."

Situation 5. Coping with the Departure of a Team Member

There are times in the life of a team when a beloved member decides to leave. Perhaps they just need a change or a higher salary, or they have a family crisis or a health problem or want extended time off. Some team members may be closer to the one who is leaving but adapting to the loss can be disorienting and uncomfortable for everyone. A cohesive team is like an organism: if one part changes the rest of the group feels it too.

It's gracious to show empathy for a team member's choice to leave rather than questioning it or making them feel guilty. Plus, it's a beautiful ritual to gather as a group to say goodbye and express appreciation. (Even if you didn't get along with the person, you can still wish them well.)

In the aftermath of someone leaving, the team must have permission to feel sad. It's also essential to hold a welcoming space for a new team member. This person will be different from the one who left. Appreciate the special strengths they bring to the group.

What to Say

"You will truly be missed. I've enjoyed working together. Even when we disagreed, we showed each other respect. We will always appreciate your energy, your input, and your smile. We wish you continued success."

What Not to Say

"How can you leave us? You know you are needed here. Had I known that you would abandon us in the middle of this project, I wouldn't have relied on you. This will hurt the team and our progress."

The Gift of Playfulness

Your workplace can be intense with multiple meetings and demands. There is often a real seriousness to it. But you can also balance that intensity with laughter and fun. Lightening the mood by bringing a sense of play into the environment creates positive energy.

Many of us tend to be overly serious about work (and everything else), so we tighten up and forget to laugh. When many of us are under pressure our minds freeze and our hearts close as a result of overwhelm. So it's rejuvenating to take a sacred pause from struggling and just relax. A tense environment is painful to work in, whereas a time-out to play inspires creativity, empathy, and intuition and creates individual and corporate wellness.

When I gave a talk about empathy at Google in Venice, California, I noticed that the décor was whimsical. The building's entrance was shaped like a giant pair of binoculars, and I was greeted with bright colors and unexpected delights such as surfboards and old-fashioned telephone booths. There was even a basketball court at another location.

Emphasizing play generates an upbeat vibe and provides a fun alternative to more sterile or simply utilitarian work settings.

Other ways to bring playfulness into your work environment, even if the company doesn't prioritize it, is to decorate your workstation in colorful, playful ways. Bring in adorable photos of your animal companions, kids, and other people or leaders who lift your spirits. Or arrange a break time with a team member to talk about nonwork activities: movies you love, art, team sports, gorgeous hiking trails, or any activity that brings you joy. This will help break the spell of seriousness in an intense work setting. Having a good laugh with coworkers can lighten up the environment too. Smile at people and affirm each other's sense of humor. It's wonderful if a team can help each other look at the bright side of work and life.

Global Empathic Leadership

Though empathy is traditionally considered a "soft power" in global diplomacy, it refers to our ability to collaborate and negotiate with other countries rather than coerce them though military action or other threats. A global empathic leader will leave no stone unturned to prevent war.

Examples of global empathic leaders include His Holiness the 14th Dalai Lama; Nelson Mandela; Jacinda Ardern; and Aung San Suu Kyi, the Burmese human rights activist and Nobel Peace Prize winner. Similarly, Lincoln's timeless second inaugural address inspires us to have "malice for none and charity for all."[11]

Albert Einstein believed that peace cannot be kept by force but rather through understanding. Wars have plagued our planet for millennia. We each have a latent warlike part of our nature, which can do terrible harm when left unchecked. To counteract it, we must realize that we are so much more than that aspect of ourselves. We must not deny our primitive instinct for violence, but we must consciously shift to a different place.

When global and business leaders model the powers of empathy and kindness, we can all follow their example. Empathic leaders value being humble. They are the ones who fold up the chairs and put them on the side of the room—not the ones ordering other people to do it. Thus, the humble power of empathy can be transmitted in various professions, in governments and businesses, and interpersonally down through the generations.

There are special times when we have a chance to undergo a paradigm shift—a grand reset that takes us to a more caring level of relating, integrating empathy into workplace and global leadership. We are living in one such time. So as individuals and systems undergo this shift, we need to be patient with each other as we adjust to a kinder, more enlightened way to be.

Together, let's support a more human-friendly way of succeeding at work and at a global level while treating others well. I hold close the belief that each one of us must embody the change we want to create. Empathy will help the world embrace this message on a deeper level.

EMPATHY IN ACTION

Be an Empathic Leader in Your Life

In quiet moments, reflect on how you can be an empathic leader at work or in other areas of your life. What qualities do you want to convey? Ask yourself, *How can I be kinder? How can I better empathize with a colleague when they are stuck and struggling? How can I intervene to relieve a friend's or team member's stress?* Spend some open-ended time meditating on qualities you'd like to develop as an emotionally intelligent empathic leader. Then get ready to put them into action at work and in your life.

The Healing Grace
of Forgiveness

Releasing Resentments,
Building Empathy

AN INGENIOUS HEALING GIFT of empathy is that it can help you to forgive someone and release bitterness and resentments, so these feelings don't deplete you. Now you will have a way out of suffering from past hurts if you choose it. Picture the lightness of being and creativity that you will liberate when the weight of resentments is lifted.

What is forgiveness? It's an emotional cleansing and self-healing process where you compassionately release smaller and larger resentments to clear unwanted negativity. Resentments can be directed toward others or yourself. They can include staying angry or vengeful when you've been harmed or when love or life or human beings have let you down. By forgiving, you can release a resentment, an empathy-centered practice that doesn't involve emotionally bypassing your real feelings. It's essential to also release your attachment to a resentment and the mileage you're still getting from holding on to it, such as others' sympathy or support for having a poor-me mentality.

Forgiveness, as I'm defining it, mainly refers to forgiving the person, not the damaging act. What do you forgive? A person's shortcomings, limitations, or their unhealed emotional injuries (whether they're aware of them or not) that cause them to be insensitive or harm others. Understanding their perspective doesn't justify it. However, empathizing with people's hidden struggles will help you release a resentment as well as any unwanted attachment to the person and the trauma they caused so you are freer to move on.

Forgiveness is more about healing yourself than changing the person who harmed you.

Forgiveness means different things in different situations. Certain people may be easier to forgive, especially if they didn't intend to hurt you or are immature, careless, or inconsiderate at times. More minor offenses include someone who forgets an appointment or checks their cellphone when you're talking. If a person has emotional challenges such as depression, anxiety, or cognitive restrictions, but they're doing their best, you can also find forgiveness. Or you might decide to give a friend a second chance when they misread a social situation and didn't mean to embarrass you, especially if they regret their actions and make amends.

I pre-forgive some people in my life. For instance, my outspoken friend Berenice taught me to stand firm with my own views. Though Berenice was deeply compassionate, she could be prickly and oppositional. Still, I intuitively knew that we would be life-long friends until her passing, which occurred when she was ninety-three. So, I pre-forgave Berenice for everything. Though some people didn't understand my choice since our relationship could periodically be tumultuous, I feel great about it.

Some central people in our lives may just be hard to deal with and probably won't change. It doesn't necessarily mean that you can't have a close, rewarding relationship with them. In your exploration of forgiveness, this is a nuance to consider.

What about people who are tougher, even impossible to forgive such as a friend who gaslights you or a family member who purposely excludes you from gatherings? These situations can feel devastating. Also, I'm not suggesting that you excuse or forget a monstrous betrayal or act of violence, nor must you keep this person in your life. Cutting your bond with them may be the best way to practice self-compassion.

Whether you forgive someone's behavior is up to you. It is a choice to respect in yourself and never force. Sometimes, though, with time, growth, and distance, you may become ready to forgive in ways you never thought possible—an unexpected change that evolves as you heal.

Your heart knows when it has had enough. Accepting that you will never get love, respect, or even an apology from certain people can help you release a resentment and offer a sense of closure and peace. You can't think your way to forgiveness, but your heart can show you the path there.

Understandably, you might ask, "Why would I even want to forgive? I'm not a doormat!" Of course, you are angry, disappointed, and sad. All your feelings are justified. However, you must decide: *Do I want to heal from this situation, or do I want to hold on to the resentment forever?* You can't have it both ways. No matter how unfair and unkind someone's actions may be, the hard truth is that clinging to resentments damages you more than the other person. Forgiveness severs the bond of resentment to past hurts.

Empathy offers you a chance to be extraordinary by pointing the way to forgiveness.

Developing the Willingness to Release Resentments

A tricky part of healing resentments is that you must be willing to release them—and resentments also must be willing to release you. Resentments have a life of their own. I liken them to barnacles that attach themselves and cling to your being. Barnacles are most known for their "super glue," which allows them to stick to any surface for a lifetime. So letting go becomes a joint effort. In response to your willingness to forgive, a resentment loosens its grip on you too.

I know that it's asking a lot to let go of resentments. Anger can be addictive; it may give you a sense of power when you are feeling powerless. Take my patient Bob, the CEO of an apparel company. He swore he would never forgive a backstabbing competitor for stealing a big client. Bob seemed proud of being resentful and developed a misguided bravado of, *I'll show them!*

Then Bob broke his hip in an auto accident. It took him many months to recover. In our sessions, he came to see that he wasn't "showing" his competitor anything by holding on to the resentment. Most likely this person didn't care about how he felt or have regrets about the incident. The health crisis was a wake-up call that helped Bob prioritize channeling his energy toward his own healing, not wasting it on a resentment. This was an act of self-empathy.

Resentments only increase stress, drain your energy, and take up space in your head. In contrast, a Stanford University research study showed that forgiveness markedly decreases stress, rage, and psychosomatic symptoms, a much more energizing way to be.[1]

Forgiveness is a state of grace. It doesn't happen all at once. You can't rush it, but you must want it. If you can't forgive today, try again tomorrow. If the hurt is recent, you may choose to let the resentment be before you even consider letting go of it—which is fine. Don't attempt to forgive prematurely. Sadly, I've seen some well-meaning people who try to jump from a crushing loss to forgiveness before they process their pain. This emotional bypassing often stems from a misguided sense of spiritual correctness, which can lead to repressed feelings that surface in destructive ways.

Zoe, a workshop participant, honestly felt she had forgiven her emotionally unavailable boyfriend who couldn't commit to her. It had taken her a mere day to "get over him." But a few months after their split, she ran into him in a restaurant. When he seemed as distant as ever, she lost her temper and angrily berated him for being "commitment phobic" and "withholding." This intense reaction surprised her.

In our sessions, Zoe needed to express her anger toward this man who couldn't be there for her, rather than skipping too blithely to forgiveness. With time, she could see his fear of commitment as a drawback that limited his capacity to love. Rather than simply viewing him with anger or hurt, Zoe came to grasp that he was incapable of giving her what she needed. He wasn't simply trying to hurt her. That helped Zoe gain empathy for her own disappointment and for his blocks. In your life, if you're not at a place to forgive, don't pressure yourself or try to rush the process. Wait until the timing is right.

On the other hand, like many of my patients, you may be ready and eager to forgive and release resentments but don't know how. You might be tired of shouldering the burdens and worn-out stories from the past and yearn to move forward. I'll describe how forgiveness can grant you this freedom.

Empathy and the Act of Releasing Resentments

Once you are willing to let go of a resentment, you can shift course and choose to view a person's damaged parts with empathy. Through empathic eyes, you can see their shallowness, fear, and pain, which stop them from loving or treating people well. This doesn't right their wrong, but it lets you understand how limited, lost, and out of touch they may be. Why does this help? You can scale down your expectations, so you won't keep getting harmed by the person.

I am moved by this example of forgiveness. A woman once traveled to Dharamsala, India, to meet with the Dalai Lama. Outside her restaurant, she saw a man beating a dog. She asked the Dalai Lama about it. He told her that we must feel sorry for the man as well as the dog. Naturally you're justified in being appalled by such brutality, but don't stop there. Now, here's the stretch to find a deeper state of empathy. *You also must recognize the suffering in this man that would drive him to commit such violence. You're not condoning it but clearly perceiving the pain that motivates him and all angry acts. The person's behavior is a cause for sorrow and grief in us all. This stretch to find empathy lets you see the whole person.*

You might think, *Sure, the Dalai Lama can have this level of understanding but how can we mere mortals find it?* That is where spiritual empathy comes in. This is your most admirable self. It lets you see someone's pain and limitations, which they may be oblivious to, from your heart. Resentments fester in the mind. Empathy helps you disconnect with and move past the pain someone caused you. You can't think your way to forgiveness, but your heart can point you there.

Empathy is a relaxing and expansive force. It helps you disconnect with and move past the pain someone caused you. Initially, this approach may feel counterintuitive, and you may resist it. So start with the smaller resentments and slowly work up to larger ones.

> **Empathizing even a little with a person's emotional damage will lessen their hold over you since you're less hooked in by anger or hurt.**

Empathy heals by offering unusual ways of responding, perhaps even awakening a surprising kindness in yourself. Practice the following strategies to release resentments.

Cultivating Empathy and Forgiveness

In Lesser Situations

Try to find empathy for a person's shortcomings. In a quiet, openhearted state consider: Are they afraid? Self-absorbed? Or overwhelmed? We've all been there so it's easier to relate to them. Then, if even only a part of you is ready, tell yourself, *I am willing to try to forgive their shortcomings*. With a receptive person, you may also want to directly approach them to resolve the issue.

In More Destructive Cases

Here, empathizing can ask a great deal of you, but it is possible. To find it, take a few deep breaths and close your eyes. Then focus on your heart center in the mid-chest. Gently put your palm over this area. Allow your heart's warmth and lovingkindness to help you expand into your larger self. Nothing to do but feel the love. Just let it happen.

Now you can see yourself and the person from a larger, more compassionate perspective. Allow yourself to find empathy for their lack of conscience or emotional damage that made them treat you—or anyone—poorly. Inwardly tell yourself, *I am no longer linked to the person through my anger or hurt.* This lets you own your power.

Be cautious about talking directly to a more destructive person. If they have narcissism or any empathy deficient disorder, they typically lack accountability for their part in a behavior, and they will make you the problem. If you feel the need to directly communicate with them, it's often safer to use a mediator such as a therapist. They can help you convey your message and keep the conversation on a positive track.

Obstacles to Releasing Resentments

Logically, there are plenty of "good reasons" to hold on to resentments, and many friends will support your choice. Certainly, it's your right to continue to obsess about an unkind person and let their behavior torment you. Or you can call on the genius of empathy to intervene.

Resentments only keep you locked in an unhealthy relationship.

Think of it as seeing a problem from the expansive view of a mountaintop versus being on ground level. From this higher spot, new insights can arise.

Expect your ego to present plenty of convincing arguments against finding empathy or forgiveness for current or past relationships. Even if the person is no longer in your life, the ego can clutch onto resentments, whereas the heart helps you let them go.

The ego inhabits a small reality and can't see options beyond itself. It's more logical than loving. The ego's job is to protect you, but it doesn't grasp how the heart can protect you too.

Be prepared to console your ego. Show it a little empathy too. Tell this part of you, *I'm just experimenting. If releasing a resentment doesn't work, I won't keep doing it.* Then use the forgiveness skills in this book. See for yourself if they enhance the quality of your life and your relationships.

Here are some common causes of resentments that may present obstacles to letting them go.

1. Unmet Expectations

You expect someone to be loving, but they're not. You think a coworker will lighten your workload, but they don't. It's important to see people realistically, so you don't keep expecting them to be someone they're not, which only fuels more resentments. Acceptance paves the way to achieve inner peace.

Janice, a member of my Facebook Empath Support Community, shared about a painful relationship she'd had with her friend Laura. Janice kept expecting Laura to act in more caring ways, but she never did. So, Janice told the group, "With great sadness but deep relief, I am backing off from the friendship." Accepting Laura's limitations was necessary for Janice to release her resentment.

2. Attachment to Being Right

Letting go of a resentment may be especially difficult when you feel justified in your position. Your ego's pride, hurt, and stubbornness can argue you out of forgiving. Yes, your brother lied. Yes, your coach pulled you out of a game you thought you could win. It is unfair. You're angry, upset, and resentful. These are all natural feelings. The irony is that as entitled as you are to feel a resentment, holding on to it ultimately doesn't serve your well-being.

3. Fear of Being a Doormat or a Loser

People are often concerned that if they forgive or release a resentment, they are weak and admitting defeat. The opposite is true. You can forgive someone (at least their flaws and damaged parts) and still set clear boundaries or even end contact. One patient said, "I'm afraid if I forgive my former spouse, I have to let her back in my life." I assured him that was untrue since they had no binding ties such as children or business ventures. It was up to him whether they interacted.

Your willingness to forgive is a sign of strength and wisdom. It lets you stop thinking about the hurtful person or continuing to rehash the episode. If your ego is unable to forgive, you can turn to spiritual empathy. Then you reach out to a compassionate higher power and say, *Take my trauma. Take my pain. Take my bitterness. I'm ready to release them.*

Journaling About Resentments

Journal about people whom you have a resentment toward. Make a list of five potential candidates to forgive. For instance:

- Your critical mother-in-law

- Your son who rarely asks, "How did your day go?"

- A stranger who dinged your car but didn't leave a note

- A friend who stood you up for tea because it just slipped her mind

- A team member who frequently talks over you

Write about whether it feels right to address the issue directly with the person. If so, journal about potential ways to approach them so you don't freeze while

---

communicating. Rehearse what you want to say with a supportive friend or therapist.

Sometimes, though, you may assert your needs or set clear boundaries, but a person won't honor them. Write that down too. Then you must accept someone as they are and have realistic expectations or else limit contact. Journal about which scenario applies to you and how you can respond productively. When you don't have the option of talking to someone, explore other choices in your journal such as forgiving their selfishness from afar. It's your choice to release the resentment or hold on to it.

Forgiving Yourself

> "Now, with God's help, I shall become myself."
> —*Soren Kierkegaard, philosopher*

The last one you forgive is often yourself. You can be the kindest person in the world who empathizes with everyone's suffering—but you may be brutal with yourself.

What to Forgive

Some behaviors include punishing yourself with negative thoughts and fears, concocting frightening worst-case scenarios, self-blame, and always emphasizing what you've done wrong. You may feel the ache of an empty place inside, an oceanic loneliness that you keep secret or may be ashamed of. Nothing needs to be "wrong" in your life to experience this tender place, which deserves empathy too.

As is true for us all, you are human. Even though you may not want to, you will hurt people. You will make mistakes. You will fail. You will be self-absorbed. You will disappoint the ones you love.

Still, an essential aspect of healing is to forgive yourself as you grow more loving and aware.

How to Forgive

Try to empathize with yourself in every situation. Forgiving yourself for where you've fallen short doesn't mean that you aren't accountable for your behavior. You may feel terrible about how you acted but putting yourself down simply torments you. It is not the path to healing.

Make Amends to Yourself

Amends are an apology that you can make if you've hurt yourself or others, a way to acknowledge your part in an interaction that went downhill. For example, if you keep berating yourself for being laid off from work, you can make amends to yourself. Inwardly say, *I am sorry I treated you badly. I will try to be more patient and kind from now on.* Cultivating self-forgiveness is a healthy change.

The Grace of Self-Forgiveness

To begin to forgive yourself, journal about areas where you are unforgiving. Then write a personal statement of forgiveness that you can repeat.
  For instance:

- I forgive myself for my marriage ending. It was not only my fault.

- I forgive myself for feeling empty, lost, or depressed.

- I forgive myself for panicking about my son quitting his job. I will stay in the present and not project fear into the future.

The genius of empathy is that it goes deeper than your anger, shame, or insecurities to the realm of forgiveness. Perhaps you were raised to be unforgiving toward yourself. Or maybe you didn't feel worthy of kindness. But you can always start now. Empathy is patiently waiting for you, especially when you think you don't deserve it. You do. We all do. Forgiving yourself is a necessary form of healing all aspects of your life.

Forgiving Others

Forgiveness is a goal to aim for. I see it this way: Someone has got to do it so it might as well be me. I don't want to be mired in resentments. It's too draining. Even if it sometimes makes me cringe to be the bigger person, that's who I want to be. If this change doesn't start with me, how will it ever happen?

Be the hero who elevates an interaction even when a person is impossible to deal with.

Forgiving yourself for hurting others, purposely or not, and making amends to the person you harmed is important. Let's say you snapped at a valued team member in a meeting: "Wake up! You're not paying attention." They felt embarrassed and criticized by this comment. To make amends later, you can always say, "I'm sorry I criticized you in the group. This isn't an excuse but my stresses at home were adding up, and I became impatient. I'm sorry for putting you in an uncomfortable position." No incident is too small or too large to apologize for. This doesn't mean that the other person must accept an apology or that you need to accept one from someone who has harmed you. But it is important to make amends (which may include repaying a debt). This helps you take responsibility for your part in a hurtful situation, which can be freeing for you. Adopting the habit of making amends maintains caring, respectful relationships.

Forgiving Horrific Situations

On personal, local, and world levels we see and experience unspeakable harms—murders, violence, hate crimes, oppressive regimes, climate crises, and more. How do we cope? How can we take action? Here logic isn't a big help since it just gets frustrated trying to make sense of what's senseless. Is there a role for empathy or forgiveness to play?

Thirty years ago, my sweet-natured Uncle Sidney was murdered while working in his furniture store Orloff and Sons in South Philadelphia. A punk teenage kid on drugs shot him for a few pitiful dollars in the cash register, which Sidney was giving him anyway. My cousin, also a teenager then and Sidney's eldest child, recently said when I asked about the murder, "My father was ripped from me: no closure, no time to express love, just gone forever." The pain he and the rest of our family experienced lives on in each of us. I also asked my cousin how he felt, all these years later, toward his father's killer. He said, "Of course I still feel resentment and pain, but two lives were taken that day—my dad's and that of the young man who killed him. Most important to me was that this man went to prison for life, which he did."

What moves me about my cousin's reaction is that he honestly recognized the agonizing loss of his father, but, surprisingly, he also had developed a sense of understanding for the terrible price that young killer paid, and he empathized with how lost this young man must have been. Remarkably, he was able to hold both his own pain and his empathy for the killer's losses simultaneously. No one suggested that he feel this way, but with time, his heart naturally went to that place too, an instinctive form of self-healing that can evolve.

A few years ago, someone at the prison offered my cousin a chance to meet with his father's murderer if that could help him heal. My cousin declined, though, incredibly, it wasn't with anger or bitterness. He simply felt that it would not be useful for him. My cousin is a caring man who hasn't let this potentially lethal wound stop him from loving his own family and others in his life. He carries his father's memory close, as do the rest of the Orloffs.

In these impossibly unfair and excruciating situations, it's entirely your decision whether you even attempt to empathize with an offender's profound emotional injuries, let alone try to forgive the heinous act. However, if at some point an empathic instinct arises in you, allow your heart to open to it as much as it wants to as part of your healing from the tragedy.

Forgiveness of this magnitude is a deeply spiritual accomplishment that you don't have to ever attempt. But if there's a part of you that may want to try to forgive, even in the most horrific circumstances, you must honor that intuitive impulse, too, which can help you heal from the trauma.

On numerous occasions, I've had patients whose parents abused them as children. Then, as adults, a parent develops a terminal illness, so they must decide whether to assist them. My patients ask, "Judith, what should I do?"

I tell them, "There is no right or wrong. You are not obliged to serve this role for a parent who hurt you so badly. Only do it if it feels right." Mostly, my patients choose to assist the parent to a greater or lesser degree, a decision they feel good about. Those who opted not to help also felt happy with their choice. So if you are ever faced with this quandary, there are no rules to follow. Let your heart (not guilt) guide you.

Sometimes, life takes unexpected turns. My friend Robin's mother, who had been an alcoholic who emotionally abused Robin most of her life, was diagnosed with Alzheimer's disease. As her mother cognitively declined, Robin told me, "Her memory is so bad she forgets to drink!" As a result, Robin had a sober mother who, for the first time, was able to be caring with her. Robin felt so grateful for this "miracle," she chose to forgive her mother for the past and simply enjoy their final year together.

Accepting Other People's Amends

If someone wants to make amends to you for their less-than-stellar behavior, you can decide whether you want to hear their apology and/or accept it. You are not obligated to do either, though if it feels right, the experience can be mutually healing. In twelve-step programs, part of the recovery from addictions is to make amends for "the wreckage of your past." Members list the people whom they had harmed so they can own their part in the hurt, apologize, and make reparations when appropriate.

Keep in mind that accepting amends doesn't mean that you trust someone again or want to resume the relationship. This amends process simply gives both the giver and receiver an opportunity to let go of resentments or anger so that both of them can be emotionally freer.

The most meaningful way to make amends is to change one's behavior.

Global Empathy and the Power of Prayer

Empathy is the medicine the world needs. We are hungry for kindness, mercy, and greater humanity in our leaders. We're tired of tyrants. It's no news to anyone that human beings have a fearsome dark side. However, the message of this book is that we don't have to succumb to it. And if we do, for minutes, hours, or more, we can always adjust course to not let it rule us.

> **It's a profound achievement to develop your heart and let it elevate your life and the world.**

Empathy and forgiveness can help us heal. Let's focus on that rather than squandering our precious time and energy on resentments. Our core values need to be strong, even when the odds are stacked against us. What are your core values? Some of mine are as follows:

I believe in the healing power of empathy and love.

I believe that even a little forgiveness can help counter hate.

I believe in protecting the natural world and its wild places and creatures.

I believe in doing good and trying to make Spaceship Earth, as famed architect Buckminster Fuller called it, a better place than when we came.

Perhaps you want all this too, but empathy or forgiveness may seem elusive in certain personal and global situations. This is where the power of prayer is invaluable. Prayer is when you humbly say to a higher power, "I can't do this alone. Please help." These are the magic words that invite the forces of love and healing to assist you. This activates what I call your "prayer body," which is the larger part of you that connects with Spirit. Prayer keeps your head in the heavens and your feet on earth. Picture your prayer body as a warm golden glow that encircles and protects you. From here, you can tap into global empathy by praying for the world and all its inhabitants.

Prayer can help you find empathy when you couldn't before. This doesn't come from effort or analyzing. Rather, you become a vessel for empathy to flow through and then out to the destinations it wants to go. Praying for the world is a beautiful act. Though a war or a conflict may persist, by praying you are sending a burst of caring to its victims who may be destitute, injured, grieving, hungry, or perhaps too tired to go on.

Prayer is a balm for the world's suffering. Still, for global empathy to be effective, it's important not to get lost in our collective pain, a black hole of despair. There is power in taking action whenever we can—such as donating to worthy causes and speaking up about what we believe in to people in public office or leadership roles. Prayer and discernment can help us clarify the situations that are ours to take on and those that aren't. Keep evaluating what is within your ability to change. In all situations, your prayers to relieve suffering will be heard and felt. Prayer is a sacred healing force that can travel great distances and bring comfort to ailing souls around the globe.

No matter where you are, whether it's in your chair, in your meditation room in New York or Mumbai, or even on a Saharan dune, your prayers can help spread hope to faraway people. Although you may not know them, they can still feel your goodwill and empathy. They might not understand why they suddenly feel better, but they may breathe more easily or get a second wind or see a ray of hope. Sending prayer and the positive boost that accompanies it is an expression of global empathy that has the power to touch the hearts of our human family.

• ● •

The journey you've taken in this book has covered many aspects of empathy. We've mapped how empathy can help you heal yourself with kindness, improve communication with others, and even raise the vibration of the world. I hope your heart was touched, even a little, and that something alive and inspiring within you stirred.

Exploring empathy and teaching it to others has become my lifelong quest. I love to build things, to create—a better life and a better world. Many of us want that. You are not alone in your longing for belonging and connectedness. It's a healthy instinct to need each other. The more we connect across the globe, the clearer, brighter, and full of faith our world can be. Remember our link to each other as we follow the path of empathy and awaken the radiant jewel of our hearts.

EMPATHY IN ACTION

A Prayer for the World

Inwardly or aloud, say:

I pray for the suffering to be lifted from those who are sick, in pain, or oppressed.

I pray for the suffering to be lifted from all oppressors, so they can learn to love.

I pray for the health of the planet and her ecosystems.

I pray for the healing of each person's heart.

I pray for those who can't ask for help or who feel lost.

I pray for the good of the world.

I pray that all the underdogs will overcome obstacles and be successful.

I pray that you and I are happy and healthy.

I pray for empathy when I can't find it.

I am grateful for empathy when it comes.

May we all show mercy to each other.

And come together in love.

11

You Matter to Me: The Power of We

If we remember those times and places—and there are so many—where people behaved magnificently, this gives us the energy to act, and at least the possibility of sending this spinning top of a world in a different direction.

—Howard Zinn, American historian

YOU MATTER TO ME. Regardless of where you are located or how different we may seem, I care about your well-being and your struggles. The empath in me loves to feel a natural bond with you and the whole of humanity, despite all our shortcomings and weaknesses. Empathy will bring us closer and lets us know that we are not alone.

We must never give up on each other or the world. We must never become cynical about the uplifting possibilities within each of our souls. Though you can't avoid uncertainty and pain, you can try to keep your heart open and aim for the best possible outcome in a situation.

The genius of empathy is that it points you on a positive, affirming trajectory. You'll always be asking yourself, *How can I be a better person? How can I love more? How can I heal?* Negative voices, inner and outer, will try to bring you down and make you question whether empathy and kindness are worth fighting for. Be prepared for them. With this book's tools, you'll know what you must do, no matter what anyone else says.

Stay close to what you care about, even the tiniest or most unlikely things. I care about the sky, the ocean, and the earth and her creatures. I care about my health and happiness and spirit. I care about my loved ones and my patients. I care about you. I know that there is enormous darkness and suffering in the world—and I pledge to do what I can to help—but I will only make this darkness a small part of my daily thoughts, only a piece of the picture.

As an empath, I wish that I could conjure all the healing in my heart and cause the pain in your heart to disappear. I want to make everything better for you, for me, and for all people who are oppressed and in pain. But as a physician, I know that healing isn't about waving a magic wand that just removes our troubles. Rather it comes from accepting our unique path with all its dust and dirt and flowers. Sometimes it's just being grateful to be alive.

Everyday empathy matters. It lets you stop to help a frustrated stranger gather all the food that tumbled to the floor through the bottom of their torn grocery bag. Empathy lets you cry for the pure sake of releasing your tears from all the tense places where they so cleverly hide in your body. How unfair it must seem to the body, to keep so many emotions and traumas pent up. Have empathy for your own and others' tears of sorrow and loss. For me, empathy feels like a wise old woman who gently places her hand on mine and comforts me. She has always loved me. I can trust her, and I can trust myself.

Empathy teaches us the power of our own hearts, and also the power of "we." We who inhabit this earth together. We who eat the same food, drink the same sacred water, and bask in the same sunlight. We who are scattered by the wind to the farthest corners of the earth. Our species is nearly everywhere there is ground and sky. We have vast oceans and continents separating us. Yet we are all family; perhaps not so united—at least not yet. Let empathy help us recognize our unity and our bond with life to finally connect all the missing pieces of the whole.

What many astronauts come to more deeply understand once they see our glorious earth from space is that we are one world and always have been. As philosopher Frank White beautifully states, "There are no borders or boundaries on our planet except those we create with our minds . . . All the ideas that divide us . . . begin to fade from orbit and the moon."[1] This realization can help us feel more related.

If we know who we are and can remind each other of this, we remain stronger together. You are an angel. You are a scoundrel. You are a gorgeously imperfect human with a perfect soul. You can know this with empathy. Don't ever forget its importance and loving power. This is such a simple secret but hidden from many people.

May this book inspire you to think about empathy from new points of view and to see yourself and others from the most tender perspective. I've presented a range of tools to access empathy in many circumstances. Find which ones most appeal to you. Use them every day.

Humans are often difficult to deal with, but we are wild and beautiful and we can grow fast into our brightness if we allow ourselves to. Take good care of yourself and each other. Try not to make things too complicated. Ultimately, it all really comes down to love.

Though most of us have never met, I feel connected to you. Connection is what fuels life, and empathy lets you find peace. With both, we can make sense of this world together. Psychologist

William James writes, "We are like islands in the sea, separate on the surface but connected in the deep."[2] We can find a better way with empathy. We have the potential to create an exciting and hopeful future. But, for now, take a moment to savor the knowing that you are "enough," and that all is as it is meant to be. Everything is in perfect place. Let yourself simply enjoy this wonderful feeling.

Acknowledgments

I'M GRATEFUL TO THE many people who have generously supported my writing and my empathic self.

Richard Pine, my superb literary agent and steadfast champion of my work. I am forever grateful to you.

Susan Golant, my skilled editor who helped me map out this book.

Rhonda Bryant, my talented, trusted, empathic assistant and sounding board.

Corey Lyon Folsom, my loving, talented partner who has been my rock though the wild process of creating this book, and always.

Camille Maurine and Dr. Lorin Roche, dear friends with whom I can talk out ideas with on our magical walks by the ocean.

Dr. Ron Alexander, my soul brother, colleague, and trusted friend.

A special thanks to the extraordinary team at Sounds True: Tami Simon, Jennifer Brown, Sarah Stanton, Jamie Schwalb, Brian Galvin, Lisa Kerans, Mike Onorato, Chloé Prusiewicz, and Jade Lascelles.

In addition, I offer deep appreciation to colleagues, friends, and family for their inspiration, personal stories, and contributions to this book. Your ongoing support has nourished me: Kate Arnesen, Barbara Baird, Carol Beaudoin, Dr. Charles Blum, Laurie Sue Brockway, Ann Buck, Sarah Beth Rena Connor, Meg Crighton-Schultz, Lily Dulan, Felice Dunas, Susan Foxley, Berenice Glass, Dr. Temple Grandin, Reggie Jordan, Pamela Jane

Kaplan, Scott Kuipers, Danise Lehrer, Cathy Lewis, Meg McLaughlin, Dr. Richard Metzner, Kim Molloy, Daoshing Ni, Liz Olson, Dean Orloff, Maxine Orloff, Scott Orloff, Rabbi Don Singer, Leong Tan, Josh Touber, Mary Williams, and my faithful Monday night writers group.

I am continually inspired by my patients, workshop participants, and attendees of my empathy training programs who always teach me so much. I'm also honored to supervise psychiatric residents as they integrate empathy into their medical training. I have changed any identifying characteristics to protect people's privacy.

Finally, a bow of acknowledgment to the twenty-two thousand+ members of Dr. Orloff's Empath Support Community on Facebook. Watching you embrace your empathy brings me such joy as you make your lives and the world a more caring place.

Notes

Chapter 1. What Is the Genius of Empathy? Becoming the Best Version of Yourself

1 Barbara Quirk, "Women Need to Feel Good about Themselves," Lifestyle, *Capital Times*, July 22, 2003.

Chapter 2. Igniting the Healing Power of Empathy: How to Stop Overthinking and Come from Your Heart

1 Sun Tzu, *The Art of War* (Chungking, China: World Encyclopedia Institute, China Section, 1945).

2 Prentis Hemphill, Prentis Hemphill (website), prentishemphill .com/collectedworks.

3 Robert Eres et al., "Individual Differences in Local Gray Matter Density Are Associated with Differences in Affective and Cognitive Empathy," *NeuroImage* 117 (2015): 305, doi.org/10 .1016/j.neuroimage.2015.05.038.

4 Lea Winerman, "The Mind's Mirror," *American Psychological Association Monitor* 36, no. 9 (October 2003): 48, drjudithorloff .com/the-minds-mirror-how-mirror-neurons-explain-empathy/.

5 Yayuan Geng et al., "Oxytocin Enhancement of Emotional Empathy: Generalization Across Cultures and Effects on Amygdala Activity," *Frontiers in Neuroscience* 12 (2018): 512.

6 Leo Galland, "The Gut Microbiome and the Brain," *Journal of Medicinal Food* 17, no. 12 (December 1, 2014): 1261–72, ncbi .nlm.nih.gov/pmc/articles/PMC4259177/.

7 L. Steenbergen et al., "Recognizing Emotions in Bodies: Vagus Nerve Stimulation Enhances Recognition of Anger While Impairing Sadness," *Cognitive, Affective & Behavioral Neuroscience* 21, no. 6 (December 21, 2021): 1246–61, ncbi.nlm.nih.gov/pmc /articles/PMC8563521/.

8 Suhhee Yoo and Mincheol Whang, "Vagal Tone Differences in Empathy Level Elicited by Different Emotions and a Co-Viewer," *Sensors* 20, no. 11 (June 2020): 3136, doi.org/10 .3390/s20113136.

9 Jordan Fallis, "How to Stimulate Your Vagus Nerve for Better Mental Health," sass.uottawa.ca/sites/sass.uottawa.ca/files/how_to _stimulate_your_vagus_nerve_for_better_mental_health_1.pdf.

10 David C. McClelland and Carol Kirshnit, "The Effect of Motivational Arousal Through Films on Salivary Immunoglobulin A," *Psychology & Health* 2, no.1 (December 1988): 31–52, doi.org/10.1080/08870448808400343.

11 Larry Dossey, "The Helper's High," *Explore* 14, no.6 (November 2018): 393–99, doi.org/10.1016/j.explore.2018.10.003.

12 Mark Newmeyer et al., "The Mother Teresa Effect: The Modulation of Spirituality in Using the CISM Model with Mental Health Service Providers," *International Journal of Emergency Mental Health and Human Resilience* 16, no.1 (2014): 251–58, doi.org/10.4172/1522-4821.1000104.

13 D. Keltner, *Born to Be Good: The Science of a Meaningful Life* (New York: Norton, 2009), 53–54.

Chapter 3. Cultivating Self-Empathy: Restoring Yourself with Kindness

1 Richard Schwartz, *No Bad Parts: Healing Trauma and Restoring Wellness with the Internal Family Systems Model* (Louisville, CO: Sounds True, 2021).

Chapter 4. Removing Obstacles: Healing Your Emotional Triggers, Traumas, and Fears

1 C. D. Cameron et al., "Empathy Is Hard Work: People Choose to Avoid Empathy Because of Its Cognitive Costs," *Journal of Experimental Psychology: General* 48, no.6 (2019): 962–76, doi .org/10.1037/xge0000595.

2 Gaslighting refers to manipulating someone using psychological means to undermine their sense of reality and sanity. The word is derived from the 1944 film *Gaslight*.

3 Azriel Rechel, "Science Says Silence Is Vital for Our Brains," Uplift Connect, uplift.love/science-says-silence-is-vital-for-our -brains/; Amy Novotney, "Silence, Please," *American Psychological Association Monitor* 24, no. 7 (July/August 2011): 46, apa.org /monitor/2011/07-08/silence.

4 "Noise," World Health Organization (website), who.int/europe /health-topics/noise#tab=tab_1.

5 H. Riess, "The Science of Empathy," *Journal of Patient Experience* 4, no. 2 (2017): 74–77, doi.org/10.1177/2374373517699267; Oliver Sacks, *An Anthropologist on Mars* (New York: Vintage, 1996); Temple Grandin, *The Autistic Brain: Helping Different Kinds of Minds Succeed* (Boston: Mariner Books, 2014); Isabel Dziobek et

al., "Dissociation of Cognitive and Emotional Empathy in Adults with Asperger Syndrome Using the Multifaceted Empathy Test (MET)," *Journal of Autism and Developmental Disorders* 38 (2007): 464–73, doi.org/10.1007/s10803-007-0486-x; Rebecca Armstrong, "Altogether Autism. A Shift in Perspective: Empathy and Autism," Altogether Autism, altogetherautism.org.nz/a-shift-in-perspective -empathy-and-autism/.

Chapter 5. The High Art of Empathic Listening: How to Hold a Supportive Space for Others

1 Jack Zenger and Joseph Folkman, "What Great Listeners Actually Do," *Harvard Business Review*, July 16, 2016, hbr.org/2016/07 /what-great-listeners-actually-do.

2 *The Oprah Winfrey Show* Finale, 05/25/2011, oprah.com /oprahshow/the-oprah-winfrey-show-finale_1/7.

3 Heidi Hemmer, "Impact of Text Messaging on Communication," *Journal of Undergraduate Research* 9, no. 5 (2009), cornerstone.lib .mnsu.edu/jur/vol9/iss1/5; Bob Sullivan and Hugh Thompson, "Now Hear This! Most People Stink at Listening," *Scientific American*, May 3, 2013, scientificamerican.com/article/plateau -effect-digital-gadget-distraction-attention/; Jacqueline B Graham, "Impacts of Text Messaging on Adolescents' Communication Skills: School Social Workers' Perceptions," St. Catherine University website, retrieved 2013, sophia.stkate.edu/msw_papers/184.

4 Ernest Hemingway, *Across the River and into the Trees* (New York: Scribner, 1996).

5 Richard Branson, "Virgin Founder Richard Branson: Why You Should Listen More Than You Talk," February 3, 2015, fortune .com/2015/02/03/virgin-founder-richard-branson-why-you -should-listen-more-than-you-talk/.

6 Jack Zenger and Joseph Folkman, "What Great Listeners Actually Do," *Harvard Business Review*, July 14, 2016, hbr.org/2016/07/what-great-listeners-actually-do.

7 Karl Menninger with Jeanetta Lyle Menninger, *Love Against Hate* (New York: Harcourt, Brace and Company, 1942), 275–76; also credited to Brenda Ueland, "Tell Me More," *Ladies Home Journal*, 1941, 51.

8 Thich Nhat Hanh, *Call Me by My True Names: The Collected Poems of Thich Nhat Hanh* (Berkeley: Parallax Press, 2022).

Chapter 6. Practicing Empathy with Family, Friends, and Coworkers (Even If You Don't Like Them)

1 Lao Tzu, *Tao Te Ching: Text Only Edition*, trans. Jane English, Gia-Fu Feng, and Toinette Lippe (New York: Vintage, 2012), verse 43.

Chapter 7. Healthy Giving: Caring without Being a Martyr, Overhelping, or Burning Out

1 Dalai Lama, *Ethics for the New Millennium* (New York: Riverhead Books, 2001).

2 Dariush Dfarfud et al., "Happiness and Health: The Biological Factors—Systematic Review Article," *Irananian Journal of Public Health* 43, no. 11 (2014): 1468–77, ncbi.nlm.nih.gov/pmc/articles/PMC4449495/.

3 Jerf W. K. Yeung, Zhuoni Zhang, and Te Yeun Kim, "Volunteering and Health Benefits in General Adults: Cumulative Effects and Forms," *BMC Public Health* 18, no.18 (2018), ncbi.nlm.nih.gov/pmc/articles/PMC5504679.

4 Vicki Contie, "Brain Imaging Reveals the Joy of Giving," National Institutes of Health, June 22, 2007, nih.gov/news -events/nih-research-matters/brain-imaging-reveals-joys-giving.

5 Eva Ritvo, "The Neuroscience of Giving: Proof That Helping Others Helps You," *Psychology Today*, April 24, 2014, psychologytoday.com /us/blog/vitality/201404/the-neuroscience-giving.

6 Larry Dossey, "The Helper's High," *Explore* 14, no. 6 (2018): 393– 99, doi.org/10.1016/j.explore.2018.10.003.

7 Tristen K. Inagaki et al., "The Neurobiology of Giving Versus Receiving," *Psychosomatic Medicine* 78, no.4 (2016): 443–53, doi .org/10.1097/PSY.0000000000000302.

8 Jason Silva, "New Definition of Billionaire: Someone who positively affects the lives of a billion people!" Facebook video, June 17, 2015, facebook.com/watch/?v=1589016824695930.

9 Al-Anon Family Groups, "Al-Anon's Three Cs—I Didn't Cause It, I Can't Control It, and I Can't Cure It—Removed the Blame . . . ," al-anon.org/blog/al-anons-three-cs/.

Chapter 8. Narcissists, Sociopaths, and Psychopaths: What Is an Empathy Deficient Disorder?

1 Emanuel Jauk et al., "The Nonlinear Association Between Grandiose and Vulnerable Narcissism: An Individual Data Meta-Analysis," *Journal of Personality*, Wiley Online Library, December 3, 2021, onlinelibrary.wiley.com/doi/full/10.1111/jopy.12692.

2 Paramahansa Yogananda, *Autobiography of a Yogi* (West Bengal, India: Yogoda Satsanga Society of India, 2016).

3 Yu L. L. Luo, Huajian Cai, and Hairong Song, "A Behavioral Genetic Study of Intrapersonal and Interpersonal Dimensions of Narcissism," *PLoS One* 9, no. 4 (2014), doi.org/10.1371/journal .pone.0093403.

4 Kent A. Kiehl and Morris B. Hoffman, "The Criminal Psychopath: History, Neuroscience, Treatment, and Economics," *Jurimetrics* 51 (Summer 2011): 355–97, ncbi.nlm.nih.gov/pmc/articles /PMC4059069/.

5 Stephen D. Benning, Christopher J. Patrick, and William G. Iacono, "Psychopathy, Startle Blink Modulation, and Electrodermal Reactivity in Twin Men," *Psychophysiology* 42, no. 6 (2005): 753–62, doi.org/10.1111/j.1469-8986.2005.00353.x; Katie A. McLaughlin et al., "Low Vagal Tone Magnifies the Association Between Psychosocial Stress Exposure and Internalizing Psychopathology in Adolescents," *Journal of Clinical Child & Adolescent Psychology* 44, no. 2 (2015): 314–28, doi.org/10.1080 /15374416.2013.843464.

6 Donald G. Dutton and Susan K. Golant, *The Batterer* (New York: Basic Books, 1995), 28–29; N. Jacobson, "Domestic Violence: What Are the Marriages Like?" American Association for Marriage and Family Therapy, October 1993.

7 Josanne D. M. van Dongen, "The Empathic Brain of Psychopaths: From Social Science to Neuroscience in Empathy," *Frontiers in Psychology* 11 (2020), frontiersin.org/articles/10.3389/fpsyg.2020 .00695/full.

8 Darrick Jolliffe and David P. Farrington, "Examining the Relationship Between Low Empathy and Bullying," Wiley Online Library, October 17, 2006, doi.org/10.1002/ab.20154.

Chapter 9. Empathic Leadership: The Strength of Leading with Your Mind and Heart

1 Jessie Borsellino, "#SoftSkillsSpotlight: 3 Lessons Oprah Winfrey Teaches Us about Empathy," SkillsCamp, June 14, 2017, skillscamp.co/3-lessons-oprah-winfrey-teaches-us-about -empathy/.

2 Emily May, "10 of the Best Empathetic Leadership Quotes from Real Leaders," Niagara Institute, May 2020, niagarainstitute.com /blog/empathetic-leadership-quotes.

3 "Theodore Roosevelt Quotes," Theodore Roosevelt Center, theodorerooseveltcenter.org/Learn-About-TR/TR-Quotes?page=112.

4 Maureen Dowd, "Lady of the Rings," Sunday Opinion, *New York Times,* Sept 8, 2018, nytimes.com/2018/09/08/opinion/sunday /jacinda-ardern-new-zealand-prime-minister.html.

5 Tracy Brower, "Empathy Is the Most Important Leadership Skill According to Research," *Forbes,* Sept 29, 2021, forbes.com /sites/tracybrower/2021/09/19/empathy-is-the-most-important -leadership-skill-according-to-research/?sh=5985f4213dc5.

6 Richard Branson, "Understanding empathy as well as the experiences of people from different walks of life is a key skill for business leaders," LinkedIn, linkedin.com/posts/rbranson _understanding-empathy-as-well-as-the-experiences-activity -6479717793217417216-lYzS/.

7 "Microsoft CEO Satya Nadella: How Empathy Sparks Innovation," Knowledge at Wharton, February 22, 2018, knowledge.wharton .upenn.edu/article/microsofts-ceo-on-how-empathy-sparks -innovation/.

8 Belinda Parmar, "The Most Empathic Companies," The Empathy
   Index, *Harvard Business Review*, December 20, 2016, hbr.org
   /2016/12/the-most-and-least-empathetic-companies-2016.

9 Mark Divine, *The Way of the SEAL: Think Like an Elite Warrior to
   Lead and Succeed* (New York: Trusted Media Brands, 2018).

10 Vanita Noronha, "The Day My Gut Feelings Led Me Astray,"
   New England Journal of Medicine 382 (May 14, 2020): 1880–81,
   nejm.org/doi/full/10.1056/NEJMp1917572.

11 Abraham Lincoln, Second Inaugural Address, March 4, 1865,
   Library of Congress.

Chapter 10. The Healing Grace of Forgiveness: Releasing Resentments, Building Empathy

1 Frederic Luskin, "The Art and Science of Forgiveness," *Stanford
   Medicine* 16, no. 4 (Summer 1999), sm.stanford.edu/archive
   /stanmed/1999summer/forgiveness.html.

Chapter 11. You Matter to Me: The Power of We

1 Frank White, "Opening Remarks at Launch of Academy in
   Space Initiative," Frank White (website), April 14, 2016,
   frankwhiteauthor.com/article/2016/04/opening-remarks-at
   -launch-of-aisi.

2 William James, "Confidences of a 'Psychical Researcher,'" *The
   American Magazine* 68 (1909): 589, en.wikiquote.org/wiki
   /William_James.

Index

About the Author

JUDITH ORLOFF, MD, is a board-certified psychiatrist, a member of the UCLA Psychiatric Clinical Faculty, and a *New York Times* bestselling author. She's a leading voice in the fields of medicine, psychiatry, empathy, and intuitive development. Dr. Orloff's books include *The Empath's Survival Guide*, *Thriving as an Empath*, *Emotional Freedom*, *Positive Energy*, and *Second Sight*.

Dr. Orloff's work has been featured on CNN, NPR, *Talks at Google*, TEDx, and the American Psychiatric Association. She has also appeared in *USA Today*; *O, The Oprah Magazine*; *Scientific American*; and *The New England Journal of Medicine*. She specializes in treating highly sensitive people in her private practice. Dr. Orloff also offers empathy training programs for organizations. For more inspiration and to learn about Dr. Orloff's Empath Support Newsletter and Empath Support Community on Facebook visit drjudithorloff.com.

About Sounds True

SOUNDS TRUE was founded in 1985 by Tami Simon with a clear mission: to disseminate spiritual wisdom. Since starting out as a project with one woman and her tape recorder, we have grown into a multimedia publishing company with a catalog of more than 3,000 titles by some of the leading teachers and visionaries of our time, and an ever-expanding family of beloved customers from across the world.

In more than three decades of evolution, Sounds True has maintained our focus on our overriding purpose and mission: to wake up the world. We offer books, audio programs, online learning experiences, and in-person events to support your personal growth and awakening, and to unlock our greatest human capacities to love and serve.

At SoundsTrue.com you'll find a wealth of resources to enrich your journey, including our weekly *Insights at the Edge* podcast, free downloads, and information about our nonprofit Sounds True Foundation, where we strive to remove financial barriers to the materials we publish through scholarships and donations worldwide.

To learn more, please visit SoundsTrue.com/freegifts or call us toll-free at 800.333.9185.

Together, we can wake up the world.